Eva-Maria Steiger

Personal Bankruptcy Law

GABLER EDITION WISSENSCHAFT

Ökonomische Analyse des Rechts

Die ökonomische Analyse des Rechts untersucht Rechtsnormen auf ihre gesellschaftlichen Folgewirkungen und bedient sich dabei des methodischen Instrumentariums der Wirtschaftswissenschaften, insbesondere der Mikroökonomie, der Neuen Institutionen- und Konstitutionenökonomie. Sie ist ein interdisziplinäres Forschungsgebiet, in dem sowohl Rechtswissenschaftler als auch Wirtschaftswissenschaftler tätig sind und das zu wesentlichen neuen Erkenntnissen über Funktion und Wirkungen von Rechtsnormen geführt hat.

Die Schriftenreihe enthält Monographien zu verschiedenen Rechtsgebieten und Rechtsentwicklungen. Sie behandelt Fragestellungen aus den Bereichen Wirtschaftsrecht, Vertragsrecht, Haftungsrecht, Sachenrecht und verwaltungsrechtliche Regulierung.

Eva-Maria Steiger

Personal Bankruptcy Law

An Economic Analysis

Deutscher Universitäts-Verlag

Bibliografische Information Der Deutschen Bibliothek
Die Deutsche Bibliothek verzeichnet diese Publikation in der Deutschen Nationalbibliografie; detaillierte bibliografische Daten sind im Internet über <http://dnb.ddb.de> abrufbar.

Dissertation Universität Hamburg, 2004

1. Auflage Mai 2005

Lektorat: Brigitte Siegel / Sabine Schöller

Der Deutsche Universitäts-Verlag ist ein Unternehmen von Springer Science+Business Media.
www.duv.de

Umschlaggestaltung: Regine Zimmer, Dipl.-Designerin, Frankfurt/Main

Gedruckt auf säurefreiem und chlorfrei gebleichtem Papier

ISBN-13:978-3-8244-8344-0 e-ISBN-13:978-3-322-81965-9
DOI: 10.1007/978-3-322-81965-9

to HMS

Preface

Mortal, pay your debts up duly,
Long, oh long is this life's vale;
Count on borrowing later, as you
Did so often without fail.[1]

Heinrich Heine (Kleine Gedichte 1824)

Lately, consumer bankruptcy is receiving greater attention by legal and economic scholars. Regulations have been substantially revised in several countries, and currently a major reform is near enactment in the U.S. This publication offers a generalized framework to analyze the impact of consumer debt release regulation on consumer behavior. The primary justification for the discharge policy is to preserve human capital by maintaining incentives to work. The analysis provided in this book appraises the capacity of existing regulations to incentivize efficient level of effort prior to distress and post filing. Post filing debt discharge is found to be desirable and necessary. Yet, the prospect of this discharge has the potential of distorting consumer incentives prior to distress. I integrate ex-post findings into the ex-ante analysis and analyze the capacity of existing regulations to meet these conflicting goals. A reform is proposed which - according to the analysis - would minimize distortions at both dates.

This is my PhD thesis and I would like to take this opportunity to give thanks to the people whose efforts have greatly improved this work.

[1] Translation Draper (1982) p. 91 (German version: Mensch, bezahle deine Schulden, / Lang ist ja die Lebensbahn, / Und du mußt noch manchmal borgen, / Wie du es so oft getan.)

I thank Hans-Bernd Schäfer for his support, His efforts and contribution to the PhD program in law and economics is unparalleled. Personally, I have benefited from both the academic environment and the opportunities provided by this program - in particular the occasion of spending the academic year 2000/01 at the University of California at Berkeley. I thank Robert Cooter for his hospitality. Also, I gratefully acknowledge the support of the Deutsche Forschungsgemeinschaft and the John Olin Foundation.

Special thanks go to Jochen Bigus for guidance and encouragement. I am also indebted to Andreas Wiggers for endless discussions and patient draft-reading. For thought-provoking discussion and for scrutinizing the model I thank Ines Lindner, Michel Robe, Beatriz Gaitán Soto and Georg von Wangenheim. I also thank my supervisor, Manfred Holler.
This work has been furthered by the comments and suggestions of the participants at the following conferences and workshops: at The 7th Spring Meeting of the Young Economists at Université Paris I Panthéon-Sorbonne, at the 4th Workshop on Institutional Analysis at Universitat Pompeu Fabra, Barcelona, at the Midterm Workshop in Law and Economics at the University of Bologna, at the Annual Meeting of the Verein für Socialpolitik at the Technische Universität Dresden and at the VOSTA Seminar at the Austrian National Bank. For comments and suggestions, I thank Benito Arruñada, William Carney, Hans-Peter Grüner, Stefano Lombardo, Eric Posner, Daniel Rubinfeld, and Branko Uroševic. Also, I would like to acknowledge Nancy Hite, whose efforts have improved the language and style of this work.

Maybe more important was the non-accademic support. I would like to thank my friends in Berkeley, Hamburg and elsewhere for their contribution of smiles and laughter, for distractions and for helping me to develop a more relaxed attitude towards life.

Finally and most of all I thank my family for their encouragement and support. And, for a myriad of reasons, I dedicate this book to my mother.

Eva-Maria Steiger

Contents

Chapter 1
Introduction

An increasing number of consumer goods, such as cars, furniture or electronic equipment, are bought on credit. Instead of accumulating sufficient savings first before purchasing these goods, consumers often buy on credit, and then pay these credits from their future earnings. Reasons for this more frequent use of credit include both a change in attitude towards borrowing, and the deregulation of consumer credit. The deregulation has resulted in increased competition in the credit market thereby making credit easily accessible to consumers. This seems to be a desirable development, from a welfare perspective, since it enables consumers to shift consumption to the most preferred period, and thus, allows for a lower constraint in intertemporal utility maximization. However, the flip side of easier accessibility of credit is that default rates have risen considerably.

Many argue that these rapidly rising filing rates cannot only be attributed to the mere increase in credit options, but rather to the fact that consumers take insufficient precaution to avoid distress. Accordingly, consumers may be tempted to profit from default by externalizing the risk of credit to their creditors.[1] Some bankruptcy systems encourage the debtor to file for bankruptcy even when the ability to paying is high. For example the U.S., which has had traditionally debtor friendly regulations, filing rates have quintupled in the last fifteen years. Due to this development, creditors have lost about $39 billion in 1998 due to consumer bankruptcy filings.[2] As a result, bankruptcy provisions are currently being reformed in

[1] As an example Fay, Hurst and White (2002) find in their analysis more support for the strategic bankruptcy model, than the one which attributes distress to adverse events.

[2] Filing rate have risen from about 300,000 in 1984 up to 1.6 million in 2002. (Source ABI

the U.S. in order to make debt release more difficult for consumers as well as to increase creditors' return.[3] Since debtors influence the likelihood of default, these reforms may induce them to take more precaution to avoid distress. The higher the obstacles for a fresh start are, the greater the precaution. In this respect unlimited liability or a regulation that offers no regulated debt release is said to be the preferable regulation from an ex-ante viewpoint, as it gives the debtor no opportunity to derive any profit from default on debt payments.

In contrast, in continental Europe until recently most bankruptcy regulations did not contain any form of debt release. There it is observed, that due to the absence of a legally regulated fresh start, once an individual is heavily indebted[4], she is rarely able to withdraw herself from such a situation. In fact, it is very rare for creditors and debtors to agree on a payment plan.[5] As a result, these debtors remain overindebted. In the German capital city of Berlin about 10% of all households are estimated to be in financial distress.[6] Altogether 2.6 million households are estimated to be overindebted in Germany.[7] This is a problem, since (as Graver (1997) puts it) "over-indebtedness often leads to unemployment, deteriorating family relations, and demand for assistance from the social services." In other words, since those individuals with high pending debt must immediately repay every Euro they earn, the rational response is to give up on attempting to repay at all. Instead they might choose to work less or even quit

Word http://www.abiworld.org/stats/1990nonbuschaptrer.html)

[3] The Bankruptcy Abuse Prevention and Consumer Protection Act has been introduced in Congress unsucessfully since 1998. For instance, it was given bipartisan approval in the House of Representatives on 03/19/03 but never passed the Senate. Now, in the 109th congress a similar bill is introduced. It passed the Senate on 3/10/2005 and is expected to pass the House equally quickly. (For bill status see http://thomas.loc.gov/cgi-bin/query/D?c109:1:./temp/~c109zi2C9N::) It aims at limiting the debtor's chapter choice by introducing the so called means test (see Jeweler (2005) for a summary of the reform proposal and Price (2002) and Jacoby (2002) for a discussion of the reform).

[4] The term heavily indebted or over-indebted debtor is often used in this paper, it points at debtors who are not only unable to meet their current debt obligations, but also cannot expect to repay the entire debt within a reasonable period.

[5] As an example, in 2002 only in 5% of all consumer bankruptcy proceedings in Germany a settlement was reached. (Source: German Federal Statistics Bureau).

[6] Berliner Senatsverwaltung für Arbeit, Soziales und Frauen (2000).

[7] Hess et. al. (2000)

working entirely, living instead on social welfare. This effect imposes costs on society; thereby creating a need for government intervention to provide regulation for debt release, in order to allow the "morally sound debtor"[8] a path back to normal life. Thus from an ex-post perspective it is desirable to offer the debtor a way out.

Identifying this necessity, many European countries have substantially reformed their bankruptcy codes during the last two decades, while introducing special regulations for consumer debt release. These regulations entail a kaleidoscope of various tasks that allow the debtor to qualify for debt release. On one extreme, Danish law provides an immediate fresh start (i.e. an immediate release from debt) to the 'hopelessly' indebted (Iversen et al. 2000), at the other extreme Italy, Spain and basically France,[9] offer no possibility for debt release (Niemi-Kiesiläinen 1997).[10]

In Germany a release from remaining debt is only granted upon the fulfillment of numerous requirements, which entail the seizure of current assets and a six year 'period of good conduct.'[11] During that term the individual must give all seizable income to the creditors in order to pay towards the outstanding debt. Most Commonwealth countries also have a period of good conduct, yet do not require a repayment of the debt. Rather, the Common law debtor is subject to various penalties and constraints and must prove to be in good standing in order to get debt release.[12] Only at first glance do such requirements aim at maximizing creditors' return.

[8] This intention is stated in many insolvency codes: for an example, the German Insolvency Code states in § 1 InsO as the aim of the regulation, to offer the morally sound debtor an opportunity to rid herself of the remaining debt. (Dem redlichen Schuldner wird Gelegenheit geben, sich von seinen restlichen Verbindlichkeiten zu befreien.) A similar intention is also present in the legal theory in the U.S. as seen, for instance, in Grogan vs. Garner 498 U.S. 279, 112 L. Ed. 2d 755, 111 S. Ct. 654 (1991) where it was stated that debt release should be provided to the 'honest and unfortunate debtor.'

[9] In Italy as well as in France reforms are currently in legislation to introduce the possibility of debt release for consumers.

[10] A comprehensive review of regulations and reforms of consumer bankruptcy in Europe can be found in an issue of the Journal of Consumer Policy 1997, i.e. Niemi-Kiesiläinen (1997), Whitford (1997), Sullivan et. al (1997) and Ramsay (1997).

[11] The term 'period of good conduct' is a direct translation of the term 'Wohlverhaltensperiode' used in the German insolvency regulation.

[12] As an example, the regulation in the U.K. until April 2004 envisaged in case of a voluntary petition, that the debtor is only allowed to keep a limited number of exempt assets, but during a two to three year period she is subject to various penalties; amongst which

Upon a closer examination, the intention is actually to educate the debtor to practice a more careful treatment of credit. Apart from the non-monetary penalties found in various bankruptcy regulations, there are several other tasks imposed on the debtor who files a petition for a fresh start. In general, two tools exist in the various bankruptcy regulations: the seizure of current assets, and the garnishment of future income for a certain period. The former is basically the regulation of Ch. 7 in the U.S. bankruptcy code, while the latter is used in Ch. 13 of the U.S. code. The latter is used in connection to the seizure of assets in most continental European regulations. As a result of various reforms, the bankruptcy regulation in the most industrialized countries are becoming more harmonized. To explain, the regulations of many continental European countries are now allowing debt release under certain conditions, while U.S. regulations are altered to make a fresh start more difficult and limited in its scope.

From a theoretical standpoint, bankruptcy regulation serves two functions: first, as a sufficient ex-ante threat to ensure careful use of credit, and second, as an ex-post alleviation once the debtor is in distress. This paper systematically classifies the tools employed by the various bankruptcy regulation systems, and analyzes their capacity to meet these conflicting objectives. This paper investigates the effects of debtor's effort choices at two time periods in a hidden action framework and makes comments on its welfare implications. A thorough theoretical analysis of various personal bankruptcy regulations has, to my best knowledge, not been done so far. Adler, Polak and Schwartz (2000) analyze the ex-ante effects of debt release on consumers' endeavors to avoid distress, while Bigus and Steiger (2002) focus on the ex-post incentives. This paper explicitly integrates ex-post findings into ex-ante analysis and considers the interplay of these two dates, in other words the endogenous limits on liability.

The paper is organized as follows:

The following chapter **2** provides indispensable background information;

are the loss of the right to hold a public office, tight monitoring and restrictions on her financial interactions. The law in most former British colonies is very similar (see Efrat (2001)). Just recently (April 2004) a reform act (EA 2002) relating to bankruptcy and personal insolvency which "..had the fundamental aim to reduce the stigma of bankruptcy, (...)while differentiation between honest failure and those who carry out their financial affairs in a dishonest or reckless way." (Brockmann (2004) p. 488). Amongst other changes the discharge period was reduced to a maximum of one year and various bankruptcy offences and restrictions were abolished.

placing the paper within the extant legal and economic literature. It is shown that despite the comprehensive literature on corporate bankruptcy, a distinct treatment regarding personal bankruptcy is needed. Along with the review of legal literature is an overview of existing legal regulations. Chapter **3** introduces the model which is used for the analysis in chapters **4** through **5**. Chapter **6** draws policy implications from the results of the analysis and finally, chapter **7** provides a conclusion.

Chapter **3** introduces the model and its parameters. Here, three existing stylized bankruptcy regulations are studied and a proposed reform is introduced. Bankruptcy regulations influence both the debtor's choices prior to distress and also seriously impact the consumer's choice after distress, during the so-called 'period of good conduct.' The model considers the effects of these liability rules on the incentives of consumer debtors both ex-post and ex-ante. Legal mandates have consequences on the contracting parties themselves, impact incentives and also effect social welfare. Moral hazard seems to be present at two dates: with respect to the consumer's effort to avoid distress, and after filing with respect to her effort to work during the period of good conduct. The interactions between debtor and creditor are analyzed in a multi-period strategic game.

The analysis of chapter **4** focuses on the ex-post incentives created by the various regulations. The debtor's choice is shaped by two conditions, her willingness to participate in the procedure itself and the willingness to exert herself. The efficacy of existing regulation and the reform proposals (4.4.1 - 4.4.3) to observe these conditions is analyzed. Since the ability of the individual debtor is bounded ex-post, insisting on payment for the entire outstanding debt may result in the debtor's complete denial to participate, thereby resulting in zero returns. An immediate debt release is found to insure undistorted post-bankruptcy choices, yet grants little return to the creditor. Moreover, a regulation proposal should be certain not to distort incentives, since the return to the creditor largely depends on future income, i.e. the debtor's economic performance. A proposal for a reformed regulation is introduced, which is based on these findings. The proposal acts upon the notion that the requirement for debt release which is imposed on the debtor seeking a debt release should respect her financial capability. Several extensions of the setup are considered, such as sequential choices and risk aversion. Also reform proposals of other scholars are presented and analyzed within the present framework. The chapter closes with a discussion and a brief overview of the results.

The ex-ante analysis is conducted in chapter **5**. Here, the effects on the credit market and the debtor's endeavors to avoid distress are analyzed by introducing the findings of the ex-post chapter into the ex-ante analysis. It is found that any form of debt release, however, ex-post necessary and efficient, is likely to distort the individual's ex-ante incentives. From an ex-ante perspective, it can generally be argued that the harder the bankruptcy regulation, the more precaution the debtor will take, and hence, the lesser the distortion. Results are illustrated numerically. Several extensions such as the existence of a collateral and social stigma are considered. The implications of the debtor's risk attitude on the persistent trade-off are examined. First by using the classic notion of risk aversion, than accounting for time dependent choice and also considering the concept of bounded rationality. Results are stated and discussed.

Chapter **6** uses the findings of the analysis of the two dates to draw policy implications. The trade-off between ex-ante and ex-post efficiency seems to persist for any bankruptcy regulation. The goal of bankruptcy regulation is to thwart consumers from becoming bankrupt, maximize their repayment in the case that they do become bankrupt, and finally to insure that post-filing their incentives are not distorted. As is shown in the ex-post section of this paper, the concept of debt release calls for a sophisticated procedure that gives the debtor the opportunity to re-enter and participate productively in the market after the period of bankruptcy. The core issue is that when the strategic debtor knows that her debts will be released, she has less incentive to repay during her bankruptcy. For this reason, the trade-off between the costs of debt release ex-ante and the benefits ex-post are optimized in the chapter six.

The qualitative findings will likely indicate that moral hazard is present both pre-filing and during the period of good conduct. The paper provides a qualitative construct used to gain insight on the consumer's incentives both to avoid distress and to work diligently during the period of good conduct. The results of the model are used to create a proposal for bankruptcy reform.

Drawing from existing evidence and logic on consumer behavior in bankruptcy, it follows that the proposal should not distort both the ex-ante and ex-post incentives. The debtor should not be overly taxed during the period of good conduct, since the return to the creditor largely depends on future income, i.e. the debtor's economic performance. If this is not taken into account, the debtor may choose an insufficient effort or entirely refrain from participation, which, in turn, would diminish the return to the creditor and cause a welfare loss. Likewise, the debtor should somehow be kept from incorporating future debt release into her decisions. The proposal, which is fully described throughout this paper, offers a second best solution that best minimizes welfare loss given the parameters. In short, the proposal calls for the debtor to repay a fixed sum that is based upon her current assets and future income. This fixed sum satisfies both needs, and is shown to remain stable when risk aversion is introduced.

Chapter 2

Legal Background and Extant Literature

The history of personal bankruptcy regulation dates back almost four-thousand years to the code of Hammurabi[1] which awarded a fresh start to the debtor after four years of debt bondage. In the middle ages harsh penalties, such as debtors' prison, were imposed on defaulting debtors. Often a defaulting debtor was imprisoned until his debt was paid entirely. It can be said that these penalties were targeted not so much on debt collection but on the provision of a sufficient ex-ante threat.[2] Modern history of personal bankruptcy dates back about 300 years. The regulations for personal bankruptcy filings were first introduced in England and the U.S. in 1705 and 1898 respectively (Forsblad (1997)). However, substantial reform is currently discussed and has been carried out over the past twenty years.[3] In continental Europe, specific consumer bankruptcy codes allowing for a partial discharge were enacted mostly in the nineties;[4] still many countries do not allow a debt release for consumers, for instance Italy, Mon-

[1] In Art. 117 Code of Hammurabi (1789 B.C.) a debt release was already instituted: „If any one fail to meet a claim for debt, and sell himself, his wife, his son, and daughter for money or give them away to forced labor: they shall work for three years in the house of the man who bought them, or the proprietor, and in the fourth year they shall be set free." (translation in the Eleventh Edition of the Encyclopedia Britannica, 1910 by Claude Hermann Walter Johns).

[2] For a comprehensive comparison of default penalties across space and time see Robe & Michel (2002).

[3] For a review of the reform debate see Bigus & Steiger (2002), Jacoby (2002), Price (2002).

[4] e.g. Denmark 1984, Norway 1993, Finland 1993, Sweden 1994, Austria 1995, Netherlands 1998, Germany 1999 and Belgium 1998.

golia, Switzerland, Spain as well as in France.[5] Yet in Italy and France, there are current reforms being enacted that introduce the possibility of consumer debt release. Efrat (2001) identifies the reasons for these reforms in a deregulation of the credit market and argues that less developed capital markets, or in countries with a lower devotion towards entrepreneurship debt rescheduling regulations are harsh or fail to exist at all. In legal theory and also in several reform discussions, the argument had been present to give a fresh start only to the innocent debtors, while penalizing the others. This means that only those debtors who suffered an exogenous shock should be given the opportunity of a fresh start, i.e. over-indebtedness due to considerable medical expenses, or debt caused by involuntary unemployment. This line of argument can be found, for example, also in the current reform discussion on personal bankruptcy in the U.S. Currently, many members of the U.S. congress have been supporting a regulation that would systematically evaluate the circumstances of those who seek a debt relief. The same is true for Germany, where during the discussion for the introduction of a debt rescheduling regulation, it was proposed that the length of the 'period of good conduct' should be conditioned on the circumstances, i.e. whether distress was the debtor's fault.[6] Still, this is not a revolutionary concept. Unconditional debt release for distress due to an exogenous shock was already prescribed within the code of Hammurabi.[7]

In the model, I do acknowledge the fact that distress can occur due to unforeseeable events, such as the loss of one's job or a change in family status. Yet, I argue that the likelihood of the shock is subject to the in-

[5] See Forsblad (1997), Trendelenburg (2000). With respect to France, the court may discharge the creditor's interest claim, but not the principal claim, see Trendelenburg (2000).

[6] The innocent debtors or 'morally sound applicants' should be offered a second chance to find a path back to normal life. As an example: during the discussion on the introduction of debt release in Germany the Social Democratic Party (SPD) did propose a period of variable length to obtain debt release. But it was in fact a more 'need-based' approach, pointing at the origin of debt: debt release should even have been granted immediately if the overindebtedness was not the debtor's fault (see Kübler & Prütting (1994)).

[7] In article 48, it is stated: " If any one owe a debt for a loan, and a storm prostrates the grain, or the harvest fails, or the grain does not grow for lack of water; in that year he need not give his creditor any grain, he washes his debt-tablet in water and pays no rent for this year." The shirkers, though, could not hope for any ease of payment, as article 52 states: "If the cultivator do not plant corn or sesame in the field, the debtor's contract is not weakened."

dividual's effort (i.e. the shock is at least partly endogenous).[8] And, if the regulation provides the debtor with adequate incentives to avoid such calamities, she would take sufficient precaution. Put differently, this paper is not an attempt to develop a mechanism that would separate the shirkers from the innocent. Instead it seeks for a mechanism to motivate the debtor to take sufficient precaution to avoid distress. The path to debt release may differ in many aspects across legislations. Aside any moral requirements, most stipulate either the seizure of the individual's current non-exempt assets, the garnishment of future income or both. The period of good conduct is usually of a fixed length and not -as advocated in this paper- determined by a certain amount. To provide a basic idea of regulations, the next paragraph gives a rough description of the U.S. and German regulation.

Under the **U.S.** bankruptcy code of 1997[9], the debtor is allowed to file for bankruptcy and may obtain a debt discharge even without the creditor's approval. Moreover, the debtor does not even need to be incapable of meeting her credit obligations. Even though a debtor can be forced into bankruptcy, she always has the exclusive choice between Chapter 7 and Chapter 13.[10] Under Chapter 7 ("Straight liquidation"), the debtor is obliged to use her entire existing assets beyond an exemption level to repay her debt but does not have to give up any future earnings.[11] If she chooses Chapter 13 "adjustment of debts for individuals with regular income" she is allowed to retain her current property, and instead proposes a payment plan to creditors to convey part of her future earnings to repay the debt - usually over a period of three to five years. Albeit, this detailed plan for

[8] Note, that the paper does not contribute to the discussion about the 'honest and unfortunate vs. the careless debtor, i.e. releasing only those individuals who suffered some exogenous shock, e.g. huge medical bills due to insufficient health insurance (see e.g. Jacoby 2002).

[9] There is currently a debate on a reform of the bankrupty regulation in the U.S. The proposal basically aims at limiting the debtor's chapter choice by the so-called means test and restricts the scope of debt release. For a review, see Price (2002) and Bigus & Steiger (2002). Still, the refrom does not alter the fundamental principles, as discussed in the model.

[10] See Wang & White (2000). The current reform proposal limits the debtor's chapter choice, in order to increase the return to the creditor (see Bigus and Steiger (2002) for a discussion).

[11] The scope and extent of the exemption level is defined by state and federal law and differs largely across states (Whitford (1997)).

repayment, the fresh start is not contingent upon the fulfillment of the plan. Often the debtor has not managed to fulfill all payments when the period of good conduct is over. In this case, dependent on the reasons for her failure to complete payments, she may qualify for a hardship discharge. At worst, the debt is either dismissed completely or the case is converted to Ch. 7.[12] Yet, the value of the payment plan is determined by her current wealth, since creditors are guaranteed to get at least as much as under Ch. 7.[13] Upon fulfillment of these requirements the debtor obtains a right for debt discharge.[14] So far, debtors have the exclusive choice between Chapter 7 and Chapter 13; the majority (about 70%) chooses Chapter 7. There is currently a reform pending in the Senate which would substantially alter the current bankruptcy regulation. Hence, replacing the debtor's choice of chapter is dictated by the so-called 'means test.' The *Bankruptcy Reform Act*[15] would abolish the debtor's voluntary choice of chapter, replacing it with a so-called 'means test' thereby ensuring that the debtor repays creditors the maximum she can afford.[16] The means test aims to put the "can-pay" debtors under Chapter 13. If the debtor's disposable income exceeds a certain level[17], she has to file under Chapter 13 and has to pay back the debt over five years. During this "period of good conduct" the consumer is required to behave in the creditor's best interest. In particular, the debtor must entirely cede her disposable income.

The **German** Insolvency Code (or 'Insolvenzordnung' hereinafter *InsO*) had been substantially reformed in 1999 and 2001.[18] Then the possibility

[12] Even when the debtor's actual income exceeds the estimated in the plan, this will also be seized, as actual income is set equivalent to projected income.

[13] This means that the 'value' of Ch. 13 is determined by the debtor's current assets. The current reform proposal is targeted at a limitation of chapter choice (Bigus and Steiger (2003)).

[14] Note, that there is no mandatory attempt for settlement within the procedure, neither in- nor out-of-court, still there are many debt consulting agencies and a settlement is strongly encouraged.

[15] An overview of the provisions of the current reform can be found in Jeweler (2005).

[16] For further information see House Committee on the Judiciary, Bankruptcy abuse prevention and consumer protection act of 2001, Report No. 107-3, at 2.

[17] If the debtor's expected disposable income - after family support obligations, payments on secured debt and living expenses - exceeds about $ 10,000 in the next 60 months, the debtor is required to file under Chapter 13.

[18] For a reasoning of the reform see Bund - Länder Arbeitsgruppe Insolvenzrecht (2000).

of debt release for individual debtors, as stated in §§ 286 et sqq. InsO, without the creditor's approval (as considered here) was introduced. This is regarded as "ultima ratio," and is only applied if prior attempts for settlement failed completely. The regulation requires at least one out-of-court and one in-court attempt for settlement.[19] If these fail, the court may rule to have the debtor's entire assets liquidated and all income beyond subsistence level over the next six years be garnished.[20] Upon fulfillment of these requirements a debt release is granted by the court.

Similar regulations exist in Austria, Belgium, the Netherlands and Sweden.[21] The presented regulations are extremely different: a debt release can be obtained with relative ease in the U.S., while it is a rather onerous task in Europe. A reason for this may be inferred from the history and environment of the countries' respective legal systems.[22] As a matter of fact, it is observed that the regulations have tended to become more similar over the last decades; European regulations have weakened, while requirements in the common law jurisdiction are becoming more stringent (Efrat 2001).

As noted by Gropp et. al. (1997) that "...despite the importance of personal bankruptcy, the subject has almost completely been neglected by economists." Still, there are a number of articles dealing with the topic, found mainly in the U.S., pointing out particular problems in the U.S. regulation. The most common theme being how consumers are likely to profit from bankruptcy. White (1998a), for example, shows that one third of all U.S. households would profit from filing for bankruptcy. It is, moreover, observed that due to the unequal exemption rates across states, consumers can extract profits by first moving to a different state and then filing for bankruptcy (see e.g. Weiss, Bhandari and Robins (2001)). Another key issue is the consumer's privilege of chapter choice as discussed in White (1998) and Wang & White (2000) for example. They propose a merger of

[19] In order to get an out-of-court settlement approved creditors have to unanimously agree; and still, for the in-court settlement a majority of the heads and sum of debts have to agree.

[20] There exisists also an incentive instrument, in the fifth and sixth year of the period of good conduct 10% resp. 20% of the debtor's return are returned to her by the trustee. (§ 292 InsO).

[21] see e.g. Efrat (2001), Forsblad (1997) and Holzhammer (1996) for Austria.

[22] As an example, consider that the exogenous probability for distress is higher in the U.S. due to lesser social security, health care, etc.

Ch. 7 and Ch. 13 in order to mitigate the shortcomings created by the choice of chapter. Alexopoulos & Domowitz (1998) consider the adverse effects on the credit market imposed by consumer bankruptcy regulation. Hynes & Posner (2002) give a survey of the main patterns of consumer finance regulations focusing their analysis on the different treatment of secured and unsecured credit in bankruptcy regulations. Berkowitz and Hynes (1999) note that people may file for bankruptcy simply to pay their mortgage rates, such that higher exemption rates result in lower interest rates for secured credits. Berkowitz & White (2002) focus on the effects that bankruptcy regulations have on small firms' ability to access credit. In short all these papers point at ex-ante effects of the regulation[23] rather than considering the welfare or incentive effects post filing. Only Zaborowski & Zweifel (1999) consider the effects of wage garnishment on individual debtors, yet, without considering the effects of debt release regulations. They show that a 100% garnishment of wages may lead to a decline in labor supply, and therefore propose a partial garnishment.[24]

In a broader view, this paper can also be related to the literature on financing instruments under limited liability (e.g. Innes (1990) and Robe (1999)). However, these papers focus rather on the optimal financial instruments, showing that a debt contract can lead to optimal incentives, especially under unlimited liability. This paper takes a closer look at the limits of liability, noting that even though parties might have agreed on unlimited liability ex-ante, the debtor might simply be incapable of paying the obligation. In this case insisting on full payment would deteriorate the latter's incentives, and hence, also twist the return to the creditor.

Closer to this paper, Adler, Polak & Schwartz (2000) have written a theoretical inquiry of consumer bankruptcy. They analyze ex-ante effects of the U.S. regulation, showing that any kind of debt release is likely to increase distortions in the consumer's economic choices and lower the expected recovery rate of the creditor.[25] Last, in Bigus & Steiger (2002) the ex-post effects on the debtor's behavior are considered, calculating the nec-

[23] This is rather understandable, since under Ch. 7, which is usually selected in the U.S., there is no reason for an ex-post analysis.

[24] A theoretical discussion of the effects of partial garnishment can be found in Bigus & Steiger (2002).

[25] Furthermore, they consider renegotiations that turn out to have ambiguous effects on welfare, but are especially valuable for relatively poor persons.

essary shortening of the period of good conduct to encourage the debtor to perform a sufficient effort during that period, and giving a welfare comparison of the various regulations. I extend several dimensions of this paper: first by taking a more general view on the ex-post situation, then linking ex-ante and ex-post considerations, afterwards taking the limits of liability as endogenous. Last, the consumer's risk attitude is discussed ex-ante and ex-post.

Before starting the analysis, two questions still need to be answered: First, why, despite the vast literature on corporate bankruptcy,[26] is a separate treatment of personal bankruptcy necessary; and, second, why should the state provide a supervised consumer bankruptcy procedure? To answer the first question one needs to consider the particular situation in personal bankruptcy. Here, as opposed to corporate bankruptcy, no decision is made as to where the assets would be put to their best use, i.e. liquidation vs. continuation. Instead, liability is defined in a much broader sense in personal bankruptcy: the debtor is not only liable with current but also with any future assets she might acquire. This usually means her future income. This is important, because the standard credit contract as analyzed by Gale and Hellwig (1985) or Bolton and Scharfstein (1990) ('in the good state pay back the debt, in the bad state give me all you have') cannot be applied; since the latter ('all you have') is mostly determined by the debtor's future income, which depends on her effort. In other words, personal bankruptcy is not simply an issue of redistribution, the regulations are shown to have welfare implications. This paper analyzes the effects of four stylized regulations on the participants' decisions, showing how the bankruptcy regulation might determine the debtor's effort decision, and thereby, the return to the creditor.

This leads to the second question regarding the need of state intervention. Compared to corporate bankruptcy the setting in consumer bankruptcy is usually much simpler, as only few creditors are involved, etc. However, it was observed that without a state supplied debt release procedure available to consumers, agreements were hardly ever reached between participants. As a result, debtors remained overindebted and mostly refused to work: both towards paying off their debt or receiving a discharge. This development had actually been the main motivation for the reform in

[26] For an overview on this literature see Aghion (1998) or Bhandari & Weiss (1996).

Germany as well as the rest of continental Europe.

Hence in case of default, there is a strong bargaining imbalance between the creditors and the debtor, since the creditors usually simply insist on full payment and the debtor has little to offer in terms of payment or future business.[27] In this paper, I omit a discussion of this failure to agree. Instead, I take an incomplete contracting view: claiming that explicit contracting on the possibility of default would be too costly for both parties, making the regulation more appropriately provided by the state in a standardized form.

[27] The ex-ante failure can probably be explained by some bounded rationality behavior of consumers and that creditors try to sidestep the possible distortion that the idea of a possible debt release might cause. Ex-post there is a strong bargaining imbalance among the parties, since bankrupt individuals usually have little to offer in terms of compensation or even future business to their creditors. And so creditors might fancy that an uncooperative (unforgivable) behavior might be more valuable, since the reputation poses a threat to other debtors, i.e. potential defaulters. Moreover, out-of-court agreements are rarely observed and in the absence of a debt rescheduling regulation such individuals stay over-indebted for a long time. Granting a debt release is a desirable quality of a bankruptcy code, since once an individual is over indebted, she might feel bounded in her economic activity even to the extent that she would decide to live on welfare or choose illicit employment.

Chapter 3

The Model

An individual debtor (she) borrows money at $t = -2$ from a creditor in order to buy an asset A, a consumer good such as a car. The credit becomes fully due in $t = 0$. There are no interim payments. At $t = -2$, when the credit contract is signed, the debtor's expected future wealth, δw, in $t = 0$ is assumed to be sufficient to repay the credit. However, at $t = -1$, a shock occurs deteriorating the debtor's economic status, i.e. she loses her current wealth w. If no shock had occurred the credit would be repaid in full to the creditor. With the shock, she is incapable of meeting her debt obligation and files for bankruptcy. In order to be excused from further payments, she has to fulfill requirements set by that particular bankruptcy regulation. This usually means that the non-exempt income is seized entirely during the period of good conduct. After that, if the individual is in good standing, any remaining debt is discharged. The time structure is straightened out in Figure 3.1. I discuss the effects of four stylized regulations on the behavior of the individual debtor, noting that most of these existing regulations tend to fail to provide sufficient incentives for the debtor to perform well. First the ex-post situation is analyzed, viewing the individual's choices during the period of good conduct. Here the individual's effort choice has a decisive influence on the realization of income. However, these choices cannot be observed and, hence, cannot be contracted upon. These ex-post findings are taken to analyze the debtor's choices ex-ante and the effects on the credit market. In short, the model involves a hidden action at two dates, the debtor's endeavors ex-ante to avoid bankruptcy and effort to create income during the period of good conduct. The next section introduces the formal setup for the ex-post analysis.

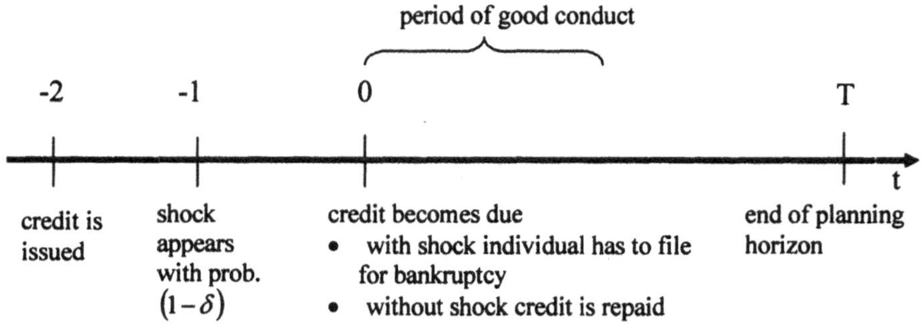

Fig. 3.1 Time structure

3.1 Setting

After filing for bankruptcy (at $t = 0$) the debtor's assets are seized to satisfy the creditor's claim. At this date the debtor has a time horizon of T periods $t \in \{1, ..., T\}$.[1] In each of these periods she chooses an effort level that influences her expected income. In each remaining period the debtor's income y_t is a random variable:

$$y_t = \begin{cases} y_1, & \text{with prob. } \pi \\ y_2, & \text{with prob. } (1-\pi). \end{cases} \tag{3.1}$$

With probability π she earns y_1, and alternatively with probability $(1-\pi)$ she earns y_2, $y_1 > y_2 \geq 0$. The debtor can influence these probabilities by choosing an effort level e_i, with $i \in \{h, l\}$ .The effort can either be high e_h or low e_l, at costs $c_i \in \{c_h, c_l\}$, $c_h > c_l > 0$. The effort level influences the probability of income realization in each period. Hence, the probability becomes π_h and π_l for high and low effort respectively.

For notational convenience, y_h is used to indicate expected income when a high effort is chosen and y_l is used to indicate expected income, when the

[1] This can be regarded as her remaining lifetime or working time. For simplicity the time horizon is fixed and known to the parties.

low effort level is chosen, i.e. $y_h = \pi_h y_1 + (1 - \pi_h) y_2$ and $y_l = \pi_l y_1 + (1 - \pi_l) y_2$

To indicate per period variables I use lower-case letters, and for lifetime variables capital letters are used.

The model is, furthermore, based on the following assumptions:

1. The debtor's effort choice cannot be observed by the creditor nor by some third party, e.g. the bankruptcy court. Rather, only the realized income is observed. However, the probabilities for the states, as well as the costs of each level of effort, are known to the parties ex-ante.
2. High effort is assumed to be efficient, so that a debtor, working for her own good, would choose a high effort level:

$$\pi_h y_1 + (1 - \pi_h) y_2 - c_h > \pi_l y_1 + (1 - \pi_l) y_2 - c_l > u_0 \equiv 0 \quad (3.2)$$

3. In each period the income realizations and probabilities are independent of both the previous and future realizations or effort choices, i.e. the correlation between periods is zero.
4. The outstanding debt is assumed to be fixed at all dates, there is no interest or discount rate.
5. Debtor has the possibility to abstain, i.e. not participate in the bankruptcy procedure. In this case she will exert no effort at all and receive no income. Her debt will continue to be outstanding and any earnings she may attain would be seized immediately for the creditor's satisfaction. If she chooses to abstain she will not be awarded a fresh start and will instead receive her reservation utility U_0 for all remaining periods. For simplicity the reservation utility is normalized to zero, i.e. $U_0 \equiv 0$. Abstention is assumed to be observable for the creditors and costless to the debtor.
6. The debtor has no seizable assets or other belongings at the date of filing, i.e. $A = 0$. The asset that has been bought with the credit, A, is still in the debtor's possession at the date of filing, but has no monetary value. It is assumed that the individual has no further sizeable assets.
7. The considered income, y_t, is assumed to be disposable income, i.e. it can be entirely garnished during the period of good conduct. Costs of effort are private costs to the debtor - they are not de-

ducted from income, i.e. I do not bother with exemption rates, or subsistence levels. The amount deemed to meet the basic subsistence level would either be earned by the individual or provided by social security.[2] Also, the effort level is used to generate seizable income.

8. Furthermore, all participants are assumed to be risk neutral, for the time being.
9. Both the debtor and the creditor aim at maximizing their returns, in particular the debtor is maximizing her lifetime income.

The second last assumption (8) is made for convenience and will be relaxed later on. Furthermore, the effects of a collateral (6) will be discussed later on. Assumptions (4) and (7) are made mainly for convenience, its relaxation would complicate the model without adding any new qualitative results. The independence of income realizations (3) might be problematic, as there seems to be an obvious interdependence between those realizations. That is that the debtor is not searching for a new job in each period. However, assuming a correlation would require highly specific assumptions, which would possible general implications. It is assumed in (5) that the debtor can choose to participate in the bankruptcy procedure. This assumption is sensible, even if the debtor is obliged to pay the entire outstanding debt in all states. In particular she might choose to simply quit working when outstanding debt is quite large. Following this rationale: if I do not get anything, my creditors won't either.

It is assumed (9) that participants maximize their expected lifetime income. This is important, as the debtor may have a 'negative' income (due to her uncompensated costs of effort) in some periods in order to fulfill the prerequisites of the bankruptcy regulation. Assumptions (1) and (2) constitute the outlines of the structure. It may be contested that the effort choice is unobservable. However, this may only be possible in very special cases and would entail large costs incurred by the monitoring party. The next section introduces a stylized version of the analyzed insolvency regimes.

[2] This assumption is a little imprecise as there is a difference between the amount provided by social welfare and exempt income. (see e.g. table of the Bundesjustizministerium, Anlage zu Artikel 1 Nr. 11, Bundesgesetzblatt Jahrgang 2001 Teil I Nr. 69, http://bundesgesetzblatt.makrolog.de) Furthermore, a differentiation would not alter the results of the model, as one may regard the additional money left with the debtor as reimbursement for costs of effort.

3.2 Conventionalized Bankruptcy Regulations

The overview section gave a survey of several regulations. Four are analyzed within this model in a stylized way. The names are inspired by certain existing regulations.[3] When talking about this requirement in general, I use the letter P (for penalty) to indicate the requirement that the debtor has to fulfill to be excused from further debt payments, i.e. the debtor is awarded a fresh start. The payment to the creditor, made by the debtor per period, is indicated by small letter p. P looks as follows under the various regulations:

- **Chapter 7:** when the debtor files under Ch. 7 of the U.S. Bankruptcy Code, all her current non-exempt assets are seized to satisfy creditors' claims, after which all remaining debt is discharged. In terms of the model this means $P = A\,(=0)$, since the asset is assumed to have no seizable value at the time of filing.
- **No Debt Release:** here the debtor has to repay the entire amount of remaining debt, i.e. $P = D$. The regulation is also referred to in the literature as unlimited liability. This was basically the German Regulation before 1999.
- **German Regulation:** under the Insolvency Code of 1999[4] the debtor's non-exempt assets are seized and during a so-called 'period of good conduct' her disposable income is entirely garnished. If she is in good standing at the end of this period a debt release is granted. The creditor thus receives the asset and six years of income as compensation: $P = A + 6y_i$.
- **Proposal:** In this regulation a particular amount should be demanded from the debtor as a condition for a fresh start. This amount is either the original debt $P = D$ or some maximum amount P^{max} that is determined according to the individual debtor's ability.

[3] To keep the analysis as simple as possible, certain differences in the various regualtions are discuounted. For example the differentiation between the right for a fresh start, as provided by U.S. law and the fact that a fresh start may be granted under German law.

[4] Similar regulations exist, for instance, in Belgium or also Ch. 13 of the U.S. Bankruptcy Code which demands the assignation of income for the next three to five years.

The table below summarizes the regulations and shows the total payoffs of both parties. Note, that the sum of payoffs should always equal $A + T(y_i - c_i)$ with $i \in \{l, h\}$. In other words the debtor's income is 'just' redistributed. The next section analyzes how this redistribution affects the debtor's incentives.

Regulation	Creditor	Debtor
Chapter 7	A	$T(y_i - c_i)$
No Debt Release	D	$T(y_i - c_i) + A - D$
German Reg	$A + 6y_i$	$(T - 6)\, y_i - Tc_i$
Proposal	$\min(D, P^{\max})$	$T(y_i - c_i) + A - \min(D, P^{\max})$

Chapter 4
Ex-Post Analysis

After filing for bankruptcy the debtor has to meet the requirements of the bankruptcy regulation in order to obtain a release from remaining debt. Here, I address how these requirements affect the debtor's choices, and how much of a return is created for the creditor?

4.1 First-Best

Referring to assumption (3.2) the first-best outcome is achieved when the debtor chooses a high effort in each subsequent period. Furthermore, since both parties are considered to be risk neutral, the social welfare function can be stated by adding the returns of both parties, i.e. $Y_D + Y_C$, with the subscript C, D referring to the debtor and creditor resp.

$$Y_D + Y_C = T\left(y_h - c_h\right). \tag{4.1}$$

Note, that the asset is not included in the social welfare function, as it represents solely a matter of redistribution. Furthermore, the constraints which shape participants' choices need to be evaluated.

An important objective of the bankruptcy code is to maximize the return to the creditor, or put differently, minimize his losses, as the received sum should not exceed the outstanding debt.[1] Therefore, this aim is proclaimed as the objective function for this approach:

[1] As it is stated in §1 of the German insolvency code InsO "...die Gläubiger eines Schuldners gemeinschaftlich zu befriedigen..." ("to jointly satisfy the debtor's creditors").

$$\min_{P} D - P(y_i). \tag{4.2}$$

He wishes to minimize the loss inflicted upon him by the debtor filing for bankruptcy protection, i.e. the gap between the original amount the debtor was supposed to pay under usual circumstances, and the return in case of bankruptcy.[2]

Furthermore, I know from assumption (3.2) that it would be socially desirable if the debtor would choose a high effort. This should, therefore, be incentivized by the regulation. The debtor would only be willing to choose the high level of effort, even during the period of good conduct, i.e. while being subject to the provisions of the bankruptcy code, if it would improve her expected overall lifetime income, i.e. she expects to improve on U_0. This is reflected by her *participation constraint (PC):*

$$T\left[\pi_h (y_1 - p_1) + (1 - \pi_h)(y_2 - p_2) - c_h\right] \geq U_0 \equiv 0. \tag{4.3}$$

The indices p_1, p_2 indicate the penalty per period with a high (y_1) and a low (y_2) realization of income, with $P_1 = Tp_1, P_2 = Tp_2,$ since the penalty can just be conditioned upon the realization of income. The debtor will only choose the high effort, if it is *incentive compatible* (IC) for her:

$$\begin{aligned} &\pi_h (y_1 - p_1) + (1 - \pi_h)(y_2 - p_2) - c_h \\ &\geq \pi_l (y_1 - p_1) + (1 - \pi_l)(y_2 - p_2) - c_l. \end{aligned} \tag{4.4}$$

The ideal rule should encourage the debtor to work hard, while minimizing the loss to the creditor. Yet, it's important to emphasize that from a pure welfare perspective that only the debtor's economic matters. The distribution of returns is non-consequential. The next section analyzes the performance of the various rules.

[2] However, one might argue that the creditor has no real participation constraint, since the credit contract has been signed in the past and he is thus, in a sense, locked in. On the other hand he may still wish to minimize losses, and it will later be shown that this becomes important in the ex-ante considerations.

4.2 Performance of Existing Rules

Under **Ch. 7** there is little reason for an ex-post analysis. After the seizure of assets the remaining penalty is zero, i.e. debtor works for her own good and faces a constraintless maximization problem of her remaining lifetime income. Hence, the individual rationality constraint (4.4) is always fulfilled, as well as the participation constraint (4.3), due to assumption (3.2). The creditor might feel insufficiently compensated, getting the lowest compensation of all rules. In other words, this rule provides an unsatisfying solution to the creditor's minimization problem (4.2). Yet, it is important to note that this rules creates no welfare loss from a pure ex-post perspective, as it provides optimal incentives for the debtor. This is true for all possible parameter combinations, i.e. regardless of the income expectations or the outstanding debt. From a welfare perspective the first best is achieved.

On the contrary, the creditor's minimization problem (4.2) is perfectly solved, with **no debt release.** No debt is discharged, i.e. $P = D$, and, thus, the loss imposed on the creditor is minimized. Also the IC constraint (4.4) always holds, since $P_1 = P_2 = D$, the amount demanded from the debtor is the same, either with high or low effort. In regards to (4.5) the two penalties just cancel out and are irrelevant to the debtor's decision. As it can be seen below, a fixed amount does not change the IC constraint and I arrive again at:

$$T\left(y_h - c_h\right) - D \geq T\left(y_l - c_l\right) - D. \tag{4.5}$$

(4.5) always holds due to assumption (3.2). However, there might be values of debt, under which her participation constraint (4.3) no longer holds. She cannot expect to repay the debt within a reasonable amount of time and will thus would choose to quit working entirely. From (4.3) I arrive at the following condition:

$$P \geq T\left(\pi_h y_1 + (1 - \pi_h)\, y_2 - c_h\right) \equiv P^{\max}. \tag{4.6}$$

Henceforth $P^{\max}$ is defined as the maximum amount the consumer would be wiling to pay. For values of debt exceeding $P^{\max}$, the debtor would refrain from any attempt to repay, giving the creditor no return at all. As a result, both parties are worse off. Outstanding debt is more likely to exceed $P^{\max}$ the smaller T is, the lower the debtor's income expectation, y_h, is, and the higher her personal costs of effort c_h are.

What follows directly from (4.5) and (4.6), can be summarized in a proposition:

Proposition 4.1 *When the penalty imposed on a risk-neutral debtor is a fixed sum of money, which does not exceed the amount $P^{\max}$ as defined in (4.6), the debtor will always choose the efficient effort.*

Remark 1 This result seems to be quite intuitive, however, it has broader consequences. It states that - from an ex-post perspective - there is always a limit on the debtor's willingness to pay. This is true, regardless of the penalties she might have to endure as a result of default, even such extreme examples as debtors' prison or slavery. Such penalties might shift the debtor's reservation utility, but do not create an additional return. They also do not create any additional return from an ex-post perspective . In other words, they are not sub-game perfect. These penalties might be capable of sufficiently threatening the debtor ex-ante, but have no benefit ex-post.

Being aware of this effect, the current **German regulation** does not insist on a repayment of the entire debt for every state. Rather they have opted to place various limits on the debtors obligation to pay. After her assets have been seized, her income is garnished for the following six years.[3] If the debtor has circumstantiated to the court her inability to meet the credit obligation, she is excused. Although she has to show remorse and behave in the creditors' interest throughout this period of good conduct, her actual effort is still not observable. In other words, each realization of income would be entirely seized, i.e. $y_1 = p_1$, $y_2 = p_2$, and she will be released from remaining debt as long as she does not blatantly offend the regulations of the period of good conduct. Thus her incentive compatibility constraint is as follows

$$(T-6)\left[\pi_h y_1 + (1-\pi_h)\, y_2\right] - Tc_h \geq (T-6)\left(\left[\pi_h y_1 + (1-\pi_h)\, y_2\right] - c_h\right) - 6c_l$$

when simplified yields:

[3] She will participate in the regulation if her remaining lifetime income after is sufficient to - at least - compensate her for her endeavors during the period of good conduct (i.e. $(T-6)(y_h - c_h) - 6c_l \geq 0$ holds).

$$\Leftrightarrow c_l \geq c_h. \tag{4.7}$$

This, of course, never holds. Simply because it pleases no one to work for others without any kind of compensation. Especially if she is able to achieve the same result (debt release after six years), from choosing the low effort. After the period of good conduct, she will again work for her own benefit and then, of course, choose the efficient effort level. It is never rational for her to generate more than the minimum level of income to meet the requirement of 'good standing.' Nonetheless, at least some income is generated to satisfy the creditor, since the debtor participates.

Proposition 4.2 *If the period of good conduct is of fixed length, the debtor will never make the efficient effort choice within that period.*

Proof. Follows directly from (4.7). □

The preceding analysis is true for most existing cases, however, it should be noted that it does not represent all possible parameter setups. There are two other setups possible: depending on D and T.

The latter case would be true if her expected lifetime income after the period of good conduct is not sufficient to compensate even mediocre endeavours during the period of good conduct. From (4.3) with $m = 6$ I get:

$$(T - m)(y_h - c_h) - mc_l \geq 0. \tag{4.8}$$

The net income, upon the good conduct period should outweigh the costs incurred during the period of good conduct, which depends on T and her expected net income $(y_h - c_h)$. If (4.8) ceases to hold, the debtor will refuse to participate in the debt release regulation. This participation constraint is more likely to hold than one of the former German consumer bankruptcy regime (i.e. no debt release (4.6)).

The other possibility would be that remaining debt is sufficiently small, so that the debtor would be able to repay P within the period of good conduct. Hence, she will try to accomplish the prerequisite as quickly as possible. As a result, the consumer would choose the high effort level even within the period of good conduct. This happens only if:

$$P \leq m\,(y_h - (c_h - c_l)) \tag{4.9}$$

Here the high effort level is more than compensated by future income. Still both of these cases are only marginal phenomena and are, therefore, omitted in the further analysis.

To summarize: Of the three regulations that have been analyzed thus far only Chapter 7 is utterly capable of providing sufficient incentives to generate income post filing. Yet, it does so on the expenses of the creditors, as it deprives them of any compensation aside from the debtors assets. Practical experience and a vivid discussion among U.S. scholars shows that this regulation provides an insufficient ex-ante threat.[4] However, the absence of a debt release regulation can cause serious distortions, as it might cause the debtor to refrain from any economic activity. The German regulation is analyzed in order to provide an example for a debt release regulation. Yet, here the debtor has little incentive to exert herself during the period of good conduct, causing a welfare loss. Thus, in the next part I search for a regulation that provides sufficient compensation to the creditor, while not distorting the incentives of the debtor.

4.3 Proposal

The existing regulations suffer from certain shortcomings, i.e. either do not pay attention to the debtor's rationale or do not adequately satisfy the creditor. Building from these observations, I propose a modified regulation. The regulation 'no debt release' was shown in (4.5) to provide the debtor with undistorted incentives as long as P is not too large, i.e. as long as (4.6) holds. This occurs because too high debt deters the debtor from participation. Therefore, it is concluded from Proposition 1 that a payable quantum, i.e. $P \leq P^{\max}$, set as prerequisite for debt release, provides the debtor with optimal incentives.

This incentive is congruent, as shown in (4.5), since a fixed amount puts the debtor in the position of the residual claimant. And such a quantum should also not exceed $P^{\max}$, as stated in (4.6). The penalty imposed on the debtor under the proposed rule is thus:

[4] This will be discussed in more detail in the ex-ante anlysis.

$$P = \min\{D, P^{max}\} \tag{4.10}$$

Note, that this threshold P^{max} is individually determined by the debtor's capabilities, i.e. her education, age, social situation as well as the general economic situation. In terms of the model P^{max} is dependent on her remaining lifetime T, the variance in income y_1 and y_2 and the costs of effort c_i. The debtor gets U_0 in the worst case. If, on the contrary, the penalty would only depend on the original debt, then the debtor might in some cases not be willing to participate in the procedure. Hence, setting a fixed amount that does not overstrain the debtor's capabilities, will set optimal ex-post incentives.

To summarize: Ex-post the first best can be achieved by setting an incentive compatible rule. If a fixed sum, contingent on the debtor's income expectations, is set as requirement for debt release, the debtor will choose a high effort level. The sum P is dependent mostly on personal characteristics of the debtor, such as her age, income expectations etc.

Remark 2 For a $D \leq P^{max}$ the debtor should be asked for the entire amount, since this had been shown in (4.5) to be a non-distorting regulation.

4.3.1 *Inter-temporal Considerations*

This section takes a closer look at the structure of the model. So far the intertemporal characteristics of the model have yet to be accounted for. The debtor's choices for several periods are investigated. At this time, I find it worthwhile to ask whether she might have reason to reconsider her choices at a later date. One reason for such a change is of course an exogenous change of the parameters, e.g. a change of the economic situation, a change in the debtor's income expectations, a change in her family status etc. Such an exogenous mutation of her economic situation, though beyond the debtor's control, would change her ability to pay and would call for some adjustment of the required payment. These events are usually covered in a bankruptcy code by a regulation for hardship discharge and will not be discussed further.[5] Another problem, however, is inherent in the model. So far, the individual debtor was considered to make the

[5] It is even possible that the debtor experiences a second shock and will, as a result, have to file a second bankruptcy petition.

effort choices for $t = 1$ *and all* subsequent periods at the beginning of the period of good conduct (i.e. in $t = 1$). The analysis has shown that she would choose a uniform effort during the entire period of good conduct. Is this necessarily true or just a result of the setting? As the debtor's only revenue is her uncertain working income, realizations of income might turn out to be insufficient to pay the required sum. It is explored whether the debtor may have reason to reconsider her settled decisions at a later date. As a result, she will now make effort choice subsequently at the beginning of each subsequent period.[6]

Thus far, I have only considered effort decision made at $t = 1$, i.e. the of beginning of the good conduct period. However, one should not assume that the consumer establishes her succeeding effort decisions at $t = 1$. Rather, she chooses the effort level that maximizes her remaining lifetime income at the beginning of each period. The consumer is now able to choose her effort level in each time period according to her expected income for that time period. P_t is defined as the remaining payment at date, t, that the debtor has to accomplish in order to receive a debt discharge, $P_t = P - \sum_{\tau \geq 1}^{\tau = t-1} y_\tau$.

Contingent on the previous realizations of income, I first check whether the incentive compatibility constraint continues to hold

$$T_t (y_h - c_h) - P_t \geq T_t (y_l - c_l) - P_t. \tag{4.11}$$

Because P_t can be abridged on both sides, the inequality also holds due to assumption (3.2), even if the overall expected income is negative. This is because a fixed amount deducted from her future income will not alter her incentive compatibility constraint.

The second constraint that needs to be checked is the debtor's participation constraint. At date, t, the debtor has T_t periods of working time left and has an outstanding payment of P_t

$$T_t (y_h - c_h) - P_t \geq 0. \tag{4.12}$$

The debtor will participate, as long as she can expect to be at least compensated for her efforts. However, due to previous realizations of income, the unsettled amount might be too high. To give an example: Consider the worst scenario: the debtor is required to pay the maximum possible

[6] Note, that these considerations are not necessary for Chapter 7 and the German regulation. The argument for Chapter 7 is obivious, and it becomes clear for the German regulation when remebering that condition (4.7) holds per period.

amount, i.e. $P = P^{\max} = T(\pi_h y_1 + (1-\pi_h)y_2 - c_h)$ to receive a debt discharge. In $t=0$ she is compelled to her reservation utility. According to the analysis above, she would participate and choose a high effort in $t=1$ and at all subsequent dates even while having an expected surplus of zero. Due to already realized income, the remaining sum (P_t) might be such that she can either expect to repay the required sum within shorter time, and consequentially receive a positive surplus. After several periods due to low realizations of income (y_2) for several periods of a negative expected surplus, i.e. her participation constraint (4.3) may cease to hold. As a result, the debtor will refrain from any further effort. She is then in a situation similar to that of the no debt release.

To preserve the incentive structure of the proposal, even for such marginal cases, several measures can be thought of:

- One possibility would be an adjustment of P at later periods so that the debtor would again be willing to participate, i.e. to set P_t in t thus that it is at most $P_t \leq P_t^{\max} = T_t(\pi_h y_1 + (1-\pi_h)y_2 - c_h)$. As a result the debtor would again fully strive for a debt release. Upon second glance, this is not advisable, as it may cause adverse effects beforehand. The debtor will take such adjustments into account. She may choose an insufficient effort and claim the low realizations as a result of 'bad luck'. In short, such adjustments may damage the incentive effects of the proposed rule. Or even after such an adjustment again choose only a low effort level, blame the low realizations to the circumstances and hope for another adjustment. Moreover, such measures would offer a wide range of renegotiation possibilities between the parties. In short this possibility seems to be inadequate and will, therefore, not be further investigated.
- Another possibility to ensure the debtor's participation is to ease the required payment to Ty_2, which she can accumulate even with low realizations in all periods - the worst of all possible scenarios. Thus, this could be set as a requirement on the way to debt release, i.e. $P^{\max} = Ty_2$. Provided that the law maker wants the debtor to be able to accomplish the prerequisites for debt release in all possible states.

$$Ty_1 - P \geq 0 \wedge Ty_2 - P \geq 0 \quad (4.13)$$
$$\Rightarrow P^{\max} = Ty_2.$$

This means that the maximum amount may only be the lowest possible income. Besides the fact that this scenario is not likely to occur, the sum of the low realizations might also be close to zero. As a result, in the more common scenarios the debtor will be able to pay the amount quickly, thereby providing only a small return to the creditor. This results in ex-ante incentive effects similar to Chapter 7, i.e. a small deterrence ex-ante, as it will be considered later on.

- The last possible solution discussed here, is to revive the intention of the German regulation and define a creation period during which the debtor has to devote her income to the creditor. Thus, $P^{\max}$ is defined as her expected income for the next n years, i.e. $P^{\max} = ny_h$. The actual length is subject to the intention of the lawmaker and is of subordinate importance ex-post. However, it becomes important with respect to the ex-ante stimulant, especially to the deterrence effect. The length of n, upon which the amount is condition, can vary from 6 years, as is under the current German regulation, to 3 years as is under Ch. 13 of the U.S. bankruptcy code. It should be noted that this amount refers to expected income. So if the debtor is lucky, she may already be able to pay the amount after a shorter period and if not, it may take some additional years. Since this is a fixed amount the rule continues to be incentive compatible (see (4.5)). However, when the debtor does not have much working time left, i.e. T is sufficiently small, she may be deterred from participation.

$$(T - n)\, y_h - Tc_h \geq 0$$
$$\Rightarrow T\,(y_h - c_h) \geq ny_h \equiv P^{\max}. \quad (4.14)$$

In other words, $P^{\max}$ still has to meet condition (4.6).
Still, in a very unfavorable case it is possible that the period of good conduct may be prolonged for a considerable number of years, if the debtor does not accomplish payment of the required sum. This may happen even to the extend that (4.6) would no longer hold. As a

result, the debtor would refrain from any further endeavors, i.e. the regulation would then fail to provide optimal incentives. Though, this would happen only in marginal cases, as the numerical example below demonstrates, it is still an undesirable outcome. Depending on the intention of the lawmaker, those marginal cases could result in two outcomes. First it may be ignored, as not to destroy the incentives for other potential debtors', or second a maximum length of the period of good conduct is set. A variable shortening of the period of good conduct depending on income realizations was proposed by Bigus & Steiger (2003). Yet, this has other drawbacks on the incentives of the debtor. This rule will be discussed in more detail below (see page 41).

Remark 3 It should be noted, that these additional restrictions of $P^{\max}$ also apply to the regulation 'no debt release.' Especially the effect that the debtor might have due to low realizations of income, here she withdraws from further attempts of repayment, as remaining debt has become too large. This effect may be exacerbated by compound interest.

To sum up: Even though the proposed reform considerably enhances consumer incentives during the period of good conduct, a welfare loss may occur in marginal cases, if the consumer is deterred from participation. It should be noted that the debtor must be given a share of the surplus under all modified rules, meaning there are limits in the possibilities of redistribution between the participants. From a practical perspective the modification $P = ny_h$ seems to be the most relevant. It places the debtor under surveillance only for a certain amount of time. A maximal length of the period of good conduct may be desirable under certain circumstances. Hence, this would insure the debtor against poor realizations or changes in her income expectations due to external reasons. Moreover, as it will become clear in the numerical example, such a scenario is only of a negligible likelihood.

4.3.2 *Effects of Risk-Aversion*

4.3.2.1 *Discrete Effort*

Until now, I have considered all parties to be risk neutral. However, this doesn't seem appropriate for a consumer, especially when her remaining

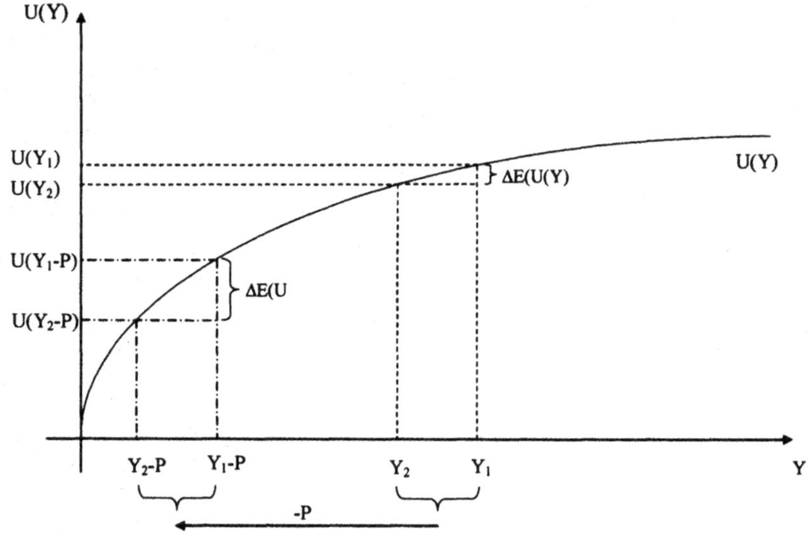

Fig. 4.1 When being subject to the provisions of the bankruptcy code, the debtor's decision problem is shifted to the left. As a result the difference in utility between the high and the low realization of income increases, i.e. the debtor is now even more willing to choose the high effort. The preceise decision problem is, of course, pictured in the following graph.

lifetime income is at stake. Hence, it should be tested, whether the deduced results above are still valid when the debtor is assumed to be risk averse.[7,8] It needs to be shown that the individual would still be willing to participate and sufficiently strive to fulfill the requirement of the bankruptcy regulation. To simplify matters, the problem is considered in a per-period framework, i.e. the debtor chooses an effort at costs C_l and C_h resp., resulting either in the high Y_1 or low Y_2 realization. Her utility function $U(Y)$ is strictly concave, i.e. $U'(Y) > 0, U''(Y) < 0$, with $Y \in \{Y_1, Y_2\}$. Furthermore, high effort is still assumed to be efficient, i.e. adapting assumption (3.2)

[7] This is important, since it has also been noted that the personal bankruptcy regulation fulfills the desire for insurance for consumers, by cutting the downside risk in case of unforeseen shocks (as, for example, noted by Adler et al. (2000)).

[8] Note, that we do not need to reconsider the objective function (the minimization problem of the creditor) since the amount dedicated to the creditor does not change.

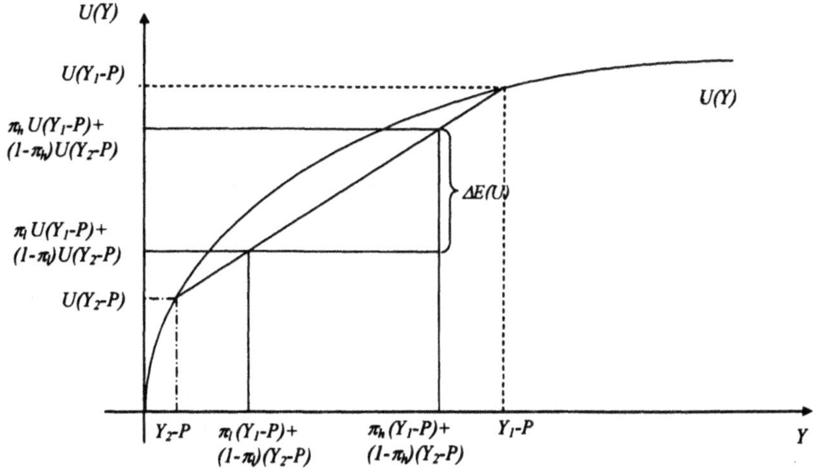

Fig. 4.2 The debtor does not compare the utility for the high and low realization, and instead compares the expected utility from each effort choice.

$$\pi_h U(Y_1) + (1-\pi_h) U(Y_2) - C_h \geq \pi_l U(Y_1) + (1-\pi_l) U(Y_2) - C_l. \quad (4.15)$$

or rearranged to:

$$U(Y_1) - U(Y_2) \geq \frac{C_h - C_l}{\pi_h - \pi_l}. \quad (4.16)$$

The incentive compatibility constraint is now:

$$\begin{aligned} & \pi_h U(Y_1 - P) + (1-\pi_h) U(Y_2 - P) - C_h \\ \geq \; & \pi_l U(Y_1 - P) + (1-\pi_l) U(Y_2 - P) - C_l \end{aligned} \quad (4.17)$$

and can be rewritten as

$$U(Y_1 - P) - U(Y_2 - P) \geq \frac{C_h - C_l}{\pi_h - \pi_l}. \quad (4.18)$$

To demonstrate that the incentive compatibility constraint holds, it remains to be shown that

$$U(Y_1 - P) - U(Y_2 - P) \geq U(Y_1) - U(Y_2). \qquad (4.19)$$

This means that the difference in utility in the constraint case (i.e. within the period of good conduct) has to be at least as large as in the unconstrained case. Due to the concavity of the utility function, this inequality holds $\forall P > 0$. The debtor's wealth position is shifted by the amount P to the left, and thus to a steeper part of the utility curve. This can also be seen in the graphs below. In Figure 4.1 the shift in debtor's decision is shown. Figure 4.2 is a magnification of the latter, as the debtor is actually comparing the utility of the expected value with both effort choices. $\Delta E(U)$ states the difference in expected utility resulting from the variant effort choices. The debtor will choose a high effort only if the additional expected utility outweighs the costs. This is always true for the unconstraint case due to assumption (4.15). Figure 4.1 shows, how the decision problem of the debtor changes, subject to the provisions of the bankruptcy regulation. Note that due to the marginally decreasing returns, the debtor is more willing to choose the high effort in lower income ranges. Therefore, the incentive compatibility constraint continues to hold. The next section states the conditions for the proposal to hold under risk aversion with a continuous effort.

Furthermore, the participation constraint needs to be reexamined. Here, no general conclusions can be drawn, as one needs to evaluate whether the debtor would be willing to pay less when considered risk averse than when considered risk neutral. This generally depends on the level of the reservation utility. The participation constraint, thus, changes to:

$$\pi_h U(Y_1 - P) + (1 - \pi_h) U(Y_2 - P) - C_h \geq U_0 \qquad (4.20)$$

The changes in the reservation utility depends on the intersection with the *x-axis* and the exact shape of the utility function. In the appendix the problem is considered with continuous effort choice.

4.3.2.2 *Continuous Effort*

The effects of risk aversion as described in section 4.3.2, become even more lucid with a continuous effort choice. To see this consider a simplified version of the income function. Namely the debtor may directly choose a level of income that determines both her costs and the overall income. Note, that the outcome is subject to a random variable.

It needs to be shown that with the proposal a risk-averse debtor will not lower her effort due to the provisions of the regulation. Therefore, first the non-constraint maximization problem is set up and then I look at how the solution changes under the constraints.

The participation constraint is the second constraint, i.e. would the amount, in particular the maximum amount have to be modified in order to keep up the debtor's participation.

Some adjustments of the model need to be performed: The debtor's lifetime income is accumulated to one variable Y, with $Y \in \{Y_1, ...Y_N\}$ in an ascending sequence. So the problem fits into a one-period framework. The individual chooses an effort $e \in [e_l; e_h]$ influencing the cost function $C(e)$, with $C'(e) > 0, C''(e) > 0$[9], and the appropriate probability distribution $\pi_i(e)$, with $0 < \pi_i(e) < 1$, $\Pi[Y_i|e] = prob\{Y \leq Y_i|e\}$. The distribution function is assumed to satisfy the requirements of stochastic dominance (STD), i.e. the distribution function $\Pi(Y_i|e)$ is assumed to satisfy for $\hat{e} > e \Rightarrow \Pi(Y_i|e) > \Pi(Y_i|\hat{e})$. Meaning that the return $E\{Y|e\}$ rises in e.

For risk aversion the utility function is $U(Y)$, with $U'(Y) > 0, U''(Y) < 0$. With theses components her incentive compatibility constraint can be set up.

$$\hat{e} \arg \max_{e} E[U(Y_i)|e] - C(e) \tag{4.21}$$

Leading to the first order condition

$$\frac{dE[U(Y)|e]}{de} = C'(e) \tag{4.22}$$

Marginal costs have to equal marginal benefit in the first order condition. When being subject to the bankruptcy regulation she has to pay P which is subtracted from her lifetime income. Thus her incentive compatibility constraint changes to:

$$\hat{e} \arg \max_{e} E[U(Y-P)|e] - C(e) \tag{4.23}$$

[9] Keep in mind that capital letters always represent lifetime variables.

With the first order condition

$$\frac{dE\left[U\left(Y-P\right)|e\right]}{de}=C'\left(e\right) \tag{4.24}$$

Here the condition changed forcing the debtor has to choose a higher effort in order to obtain the same marginal utility. This is also clarified by the graph (Figure 4.3.) below. The ascending function represents a sample of the marginal cost curve, while the others represent the marginal utility. The left line pictures the unconstraint case and the right shows the debtor is subject to the penalty during the period of good conduct. Compared to the unconstrained case, the debtor will choose a higher effort resulting in a higher marginal benefit as well as higher marginal costs.

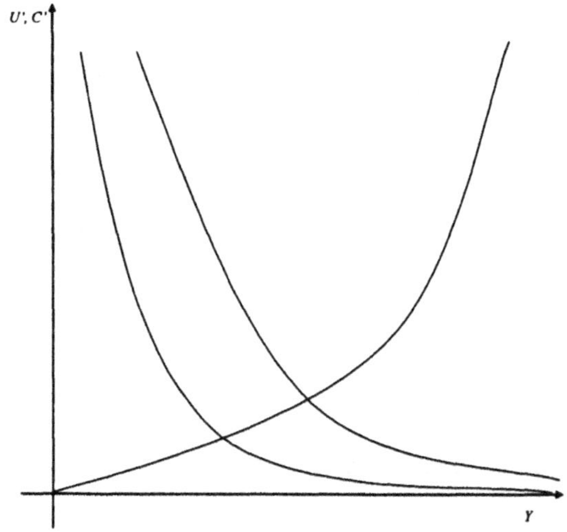

Fig. 4.3 It can be seen that the debtor will choose a higher effort so that both marginal costs and marginal utility rise.

Instead of decreasing effort, the debtor will try even harder to accumulate the necessary money to satisfy the requirement. This effect might lead to the conjecture that the effort of the debtor can be infinitely increased by raising the penalty. Still, this effect is strictly bounded, since the participation constraint is tightened.

When the debtor is not subject to the period of good conduct her participation constraint looks like:

$$\pi_i(e)\,U(Y_i) - C_i(e) \geq U_0. \tag{4.25}$$

And it changes to

$$\pi_i(\hat{e})\,U(Y_i - P) - C_i(\hat{e}) \geq U_0 = 0 \tag{4.26}$$

with the penalty. This can be also be expressed as a maximal penalty $P^{\max}$

$$Y_i - U^{-1}\left(\frac{C_i(\hat{e})}{\pi_i(\hat{e})}\right) \geq P \equiv P^{\max} \tag{4.27}$$

This says that the penalty may not exceed the income minus some term. This term expresses the costs of effort divided by the resulting probability of good realization of income. Both terms are increasing in e, while $\pi_i(\hat{e}) < 1$ making the whole fraction larger than 1. The inverse of a risk averse utility function is an increasing or exponential function (i.e. $\left(U^{-1}\right)'' > 0$). Therefore, the term increased rather sharply for higher effort, thereby strengthening the participation constraint. The higher the effort the more the debtor needs to be given in order to participate.

To resume: When the penalty is a fixed amount and the debtor is risk averse, she will continue to work hard during the period of good conduct. However, the amount demanded from the debtor may need to be lowered to ensure her participation.

4.4 Other Reform Proposals

Consumer bankruptcy receives accretive attention from legal and economic scholars. In the U.S. a legal reform is pending. Recently, many European countries have carried out substantial reforms of their consumer bankruptcy regulation. There are several other reform proposals discussed among scholars. In this section, the impact of these proposals on ex-post incentives is analyzed within the prescribed model.

As mentioned in the introduction, most of the discussion is concerned with ex-ante effects preventing the debtor from defaulting maliciously, or taking advantage of the generous discharge regulations. This is hardly surprising as Chapter 7, which was shown to have no ex-post effects on the debtor's working incentives, is the predominant regulation in the U.S. For example, the pending reform in the U.S. aims to increase the creditors' return by introducing the so-called 'means-test.' This means tests forces the debtor into Chapter 13 if her expected disposable income exceeds $ 10,000 in the next 60 months. Even the reformed version of U.S. Chapter 13 offers similar ex-post incentives to the period of good conduct known in the German regulation. In both cases, the income above some subsistence level is entirely garnished for a fixed period. Hence, as shown for the German regulation, the debtor will hardly exert herself above the level necessary avoid offending the provision of the period of good conduct.

Another reform proposal brought forward by Wang & White (2000) proposes a merger of Chapter 7 and 13. Hence, the debtor will not only be deprived of her assets during bankruptcy, but has to give up part of her future income as a sort of 'bankruptcy tax.' They show that this would prevent strategic behavior, namely it deters the debtor from shifting assets in order to exempt property. They note, that an income garnishment might decrease labor supply to a minor extent. This is hardly surprising, as the consumers are taking all decisions at the beginning, i.e. they are not allowed to adjust their working intensity after bankruptcy. Wang & White do not explicitly state whether income should be garnished for a fixed period, or if just a percentage of income is garnished. The effects of a garnishment for a fixed period have been discussed. Now, the effects of a partial garnishment are discussed in this section.

This section details the effects of two reform proposals in the light of the period of good conduct as known in many Common law countries. The reform proposal by Bigus & Steiger (2002) suggests a variable period of good conduct, where the length is contingent on the creditor's return. The idea is related to the proposal in this paper, but has some differences as it will be explained below. The second reform proposal to be analyzed, was brought forward by Zaborowski & Zweifel (1999), who suggest a partial wage garnishment to improve working incentives. The analysis shows that such a regulation is only capable of a marginal improvement, accompanied by expenses to the creditors and further distortions. Last, the U.K. form of a period of good conduct is discussed. Here, instead of a wage garnishment for a fixed period, the debtor has to endure a period of supervision, where she experiences several obstacles while being educated to handle credit. The effects of such a supervision and of the stigma of bankruptcy are discussed. This is shown to be useful, especially when the returns created by wage garnishment are weighted against the costs of such procedures. It can also be seen in relation to the insurance function of the bankruptcy code. It relieves the consumer of the unsettled debt, while imposing a penalty regardless of her economic situation. This penalty may state a sufficient ex-ante threat, while the debt release fulfills the insurance function. In this respect, the stigma of defaulting on one's debt can also prove to be useful to prevent the abuse of debt release regulation. Such benefits of a the threat of stigma will be discussed in more detail in the ex-ante section. Also, I briefly discuss the effects of stigma during the period of good conduct.

4.4.1 *Variable Period of Good Conduct*

Bigus & Steiger (2003) proposed a variable period of good conduct as a device in a consumer debt release procedure. The idea is as follows: if the consumer is obliged to pay a predetermined amount of money R within a given time limit, the period of good conduct abridged, otherwise the period is prolonged. However, the debtor is released from debt after a maximum length of m years, regardless of the return to the creditor.

Instead of a period of repayment, as under Ch. 13 of the U.S. bankruptcy code, a specific requirement R is set for the consumer to pay in order to be eligible for debt release. R is calculated as the level that the consumer may be expected to earn within the period of good conduct, $R = (m - r)\, y_h$. Where m denotes the prolonged period of good conduct, while $m - r$ for the shorter period (r for "reduction" or "rewarding"), with $0 < r < m < T$. The length of the period is dependent on the return generated and thus, on the consumer's effort level. It had been shown (see (4.5)) that a fixed sum sets optimal incentives for the debtor's effort decision. As the debtor is bankrupt and has no further valuable belongings, it is necessary to determine the amount by her capabilities, otherwise she will either quit working entirely or choose an inefficiently low effort level. As a result R is also confined to the debtor's maximum ability to pay, as calculated in (4.6), in order to ensure the debtor's participation. R is set as her expected income for the next m years, i.e. $R = my_l$. This leaves the consumer the freedom to take only $m - r$ years when choosing a high effort level, allowing $R = (m - r)\, y_h$. To ensure participation, the amount is limited to the following condition

$$T(y_h - c_h) - R \geq U_0 = 0 \qquad (4.28)$$
$$\Rightarrow (T - (m - r))\, y_h - Tc_h \geq 0.$$

Condition (4.28) depends the remaining length of her working time, T, which is a function of her capacity defined by her education, income expectations, and economic situation. Note, the debtor's ability to pay is bounded and needs to be taken into account when constructing a requirement for debt release. So at the beginning of the period of good conduct in $t = 2$, the debtor faces the same incentive compatibility constraint as with any fixed sum:

$$(T - (m - r))\, y_h - Tc_h \geq (T - m)(y_h - c_h) - mc_l. \qquad (4.29)$$

Substituting $(m - r)\, y_h = my_l = R$ into the relation again leads to:

$$m(y_h - c_h) \geq m(y_l - c_l) \qquad (4.30)$$

which holds by assumption (3.2). The incentive compatibility constraint always holds, since the consumer is obliged to pay the same amount with either effort level. The first-best is likely to be achieved as the regulation leaves the consumer as the residual claimant of her income.

However, this is true only in $t = 1$, i.e. the of beginning of the good conduct period. Do not assume that the consumer establishes her succeeding effort decisions at $t = 1$. Afterwards, the debtor must decide at $t, \forall t \geq 1$, if high effort is profitable, or it would be better for her simply to 'wait', i.e. to choose the low effort and wait for the period of good conduct to pass. The consumer will choose her effort level in each time period, c_i, according to her expected income, R, for that time period.

Since all the parameters used for the determination of R refer to expected income, the actual realizations of income may enable the consumer to earn R within a shorter period than $m - r$. To the detriment of the consumer, it is possible that earning R could take as many as m years to earn.

Consider the following scenario: At the beginning of each period t the consumer has a remaining debt of R_t. The debtor then calculates the benefit r_t of high effort. Throughout the period of good conduct the consumer owes the remaining R_t, to the creditors at the start of each period t. The consumer uses her knowledge of R_t to calculate the potential discount on her repayment period r_t and compares its benefit to that of consuming the maximum remaining length, m_t. Her effort level is determined by her comparison of the perceived benefits from the two options respectively. Note, that only at the beginning of the period of good conduct (at $t = 0$) will the equation $R_t = (m_t - r_t)\, y_h = m_t y_l$ hold. Later, due to previous income realizations the remaining amount R_t is adjusted, i.e. the first equation $R_t = (m_t - r_t)\, y_h$ remains true, while the latter is subject to change. Due to assumption (3.2), the consumer will always repay R_t more quickly when exerting a high level of effort that with a lower effort level. However, since the length of the period of good conduct is truncated to a maximum of m years, the consumer may at some point be better off by choosing c_l and 'wait' during the remaining time. Reconsider (4.29) as the decision taken by the consumer at a particular date t within the period of good conduct.

$$(T-(m_t-r_t))(y_h-c_h)-(m_t-r_t)c_h \geq (T-m_t)(y_h-c_h)-m_t c_l \quad (4.31)$$

which gives when solved for r_t :

$$r_t \geq \frac{m_t\,(c_h - c_l)}{y_h}. \quad (4.32)$$

If the expected shortening of the period of good conduct is sufficient the debtor will choose the high effort, otherwise she will only choose the low effort. As long as (4.32) holds, the consumer will be better off choosing a high effort level. When the expected discount on the period of good conduct no longer offsets the additional costs of high effort the consumer switches to a low effort, and will do so for the remaining time in the period of good conduct.

The expected reduction r_t should vary positively with the additional costs of high effort $(c_h - c_l)$ and negatively with the discount $(r_t y_h)$, i.e. to maximize the advantage from a reduction of the period of good conduct. After debt is discharged, the consumer works for her own good and will choose c_h.

Still, it may be possible that due to inadvertently low income realizations for several periods, the consumer remains in the period of good conduct for a disproportional time. Which suggests the provision of a maximum length to insure that against this a maximum should be set on the period of good conduct. This insurance role is in line with the intention of many scholars,[10] who believe that the bankruptcy code should provide consumers insurance against bad income realizations. Though this intention usually points at ex-ante incentives, it also applies to ex-post considerations.

One drawback of the proposed variable period of good conduct is that the incentive structure is heavily dependent on the setup. Here effort is assumed to be binary. In actually it might be difficult to distinguish between the expected return under high and low effort. However, approximations can be found, and this rule would clearly enhance incentives compared e.g. to the current German regulation.

To sum up: Giving the debtor the prospect to shorten the period of good conduct is a useful device to enhance her incentives to exert herself during that period. Though the debtor might choose an insufficient effort in later periods, her incentives are considerably improved for most possible parameter environments. Yet, a truncated period of good conduct might alleviate certain cases of undue hardship. Thus, the return to the creditor is increased and the social loss is diminished

4.4.2 *Partial Garnishment*

Another reform proposal which will be discussed here, was brought up by Zaborowski and Zweifel (1999). Acknowledging the relation between income creation and the returns left with the consumer, they argue a partial garnishment of proceeds would provide a better incentive to the debtor. The German regulation for income garnishment has similar provisions.[11,12] Zaborowski and Zweifel discuss the possibility of partial wage garnishment in two circumstances; either as a wage garnishment until the debt is fully paid or as a means in a bankruptcy procedure. The current German reg-

[10] see e.g. Posner (1999).

[11] See table of the Bundesjustizministerium (Bundesgesetzblatt Jahrgang 2001 Teil I Nr. 69, ausgeg. Bonn 19.Dezember 2001, http://bundesgesetzblatt.makrolog.de) The garnishment rate rises at a smaller percentage than the income.

[12] Wage garnishment can occur before bankruptcy, when the debtor is unwilling to pay the creditor can file a plea for wage garnishment. Any amount exceeding a particular level (which is slightly more than subsistence level) will than be transferred directly to the creditor, until the debt is fully paid.

ulation could be modified as an example of the latter, if rather than a full garnishment of wage for six years there is a partial garnishment for say nine years at a rate of about 60% or 70%. They claim that this motivates the debtor to work hard during the period of good conduct. Although this policy requires a lengthened period, its success would decrease the welfare loss chronic to the current German bankruptcy regime. And the creditors expected compensation is likely to outweigh the inconvenience of a longer repayment period. Note that the idea of partial wage garnishment was already instituted in 1195 in medieval Venice, there -when the debtor's real property did not suffice- future income was garnished at a rate of one third until all creditors were paid in full.[13]

In this section their proposal is discussed and evaluated in context to the model that is used in this paper. Partial garnishment is interpreted in two ways, either like no debt release where income is partially garnished until the entire debt is paid off; or like the current German regulation, as a partial garnishment for a fixed number of years. It transpires that - compared to existing regulations - a partial garnishment rule is only capable of limited improvements. The reason for this incapacity can be accounted to the fact that the success of a particular garnishment rate is highly dependent on the debtor's personal characteristics, and that a reduced garnishment rate benefits the debtor only in that very period. These results are illustrated in a numerical example at the end of the section.

Hence, according to the proposal, as brought forward by Zaborowski and Zweifel (1999), instead of a 100% garnishment of the debtor's income, it is only seized at a reduced rate of τ, with $\tau \in [0,1]$. This is now discussed in two variations:

(1) a partial garnishment for a fixed number of n years $P = n\tau y_t$.
(2) a partial garnishment until the entire debt, i.e. $P = D$ is paid.

First, let's examine whether (1) is capable of improving the debtor's incentives in contrast to the current German regulation. Namely, whether (1) is capable of incentivizing high effort during the period of good conduct. Thus, rather than of a 100% garnishment of m years, the consumer's earnings are now only partially garnished a rate τ for n years, with $n > m$. The period of good conduct will most likely need to be prolonged in order

[13] See Dandolo (1901)

to provide the creditor with an equivalent rate as the current German regulation. As τ is the rate at which income is garnished, hence, the fraction $(1-\tau)\,y_t$ rests with the debtor in each period. She would choose a high effort during the period of good conduct only if her incentive compatibility constraint holds:

$$(T-n)y_h + (1-\tau)\,ny_h - Tc_h \;\geq\; (T-n)(y_h - c_h) + (1-\tau)\,ny_l - nc_l \tag{4.33}$$

which can be rearranged to

$$(1-\tau)\,y_h - c_h \geq (1-\tau)\,y_l - c_l. \tag{4.34}$$

The consumer's effort decision may be entirely dependent on the fraction of income $(1-\tau)\,y_t$ remaining in that period. This implies that the total length of the period of good conduct is irrelevant to her effort decision. This is rather straight forward, as a higher return in one period does not alter the duration of the period of good conduct. What only matters is that the proceeds of that period sufficiently compensate the additional costs of choosing high effort. In order to insure optimal effort during the period of good conduct, the garnishment rate needs to be rather low. This is because the percentage of income $(1-\tau)\,y_t$, which rests with the consumer has to compensate her for the additional effort. In order to provide the creditor with an equivalent compensation rate of other prevailing regulation, the period of good conduct needs to be considerably prolonged. The maximum garnishment rate $\overline{\tau}$ that can be taken from the debtor, is deduced by rearranging (4.34).

$$\tau \leq 1 - \frac{c_h - c_l}{y_h - y_l} \equiv \overline{\tau} \tag{4.35}$$

(4.35) is equal to the maximum fraction of income that may be taken from the consumer, while remaining at the efficient effort level. For most parameters a garnishment rate $\tau \leq \overline{\tau}$ will also ensure participation of the debtor. Yet, this condition is not sufficient to insure participation. It is possible that a garnishment rate of $\overline{\tau}$ does not compensate the debtor fully for her costs, i.e. $(1-\overline{\tau})\,y_h - c_h \leq 0$. In this case the debtor can either be compensated by the prospect of future income after the period of good conduct, or by lowering the garnishment rate. These two modifications are now shortly discussed:

Condition (4.34) does not ensure that she receives a positive income in each period, as, within certain parameters, the debtor does not receive a strictly positive income in each period, i.e. $(1-\overline{\tau})\,y_h - c_h \leq 0$. Though, she receives some fraction of her income during the period of good conduct, this may not fully compensated for costs of effort. So she might still choose to abstain, particularly if little working time remains after the period of good conduct. Hence, to implement high effort level, her participation constraint also needs to hold

$$n\,(1-\overline{\tau})\,y_h + (T-m)\,y_h - Tc_h \geq 0. \tag{4.36}$$

In this case, the debtor is compensated with income of later periods for her endeavours during the period of good conduct . Hence, it is ensured that she participates. If the incentive compatibility and the participation constraint hold, the debtor will choose the efficient effort level.

Her participation constraint as outlined in (4.36) may fail to hold, so that her endeavors during the garnishment period are not compensated by future income. Yet, her participation may still be achieved by lowering τ so that she receives a positive fraction in each period. In other words, the debtor's participation constraint needs to hold in each period. This τ is defined as $\overline{\overline{\tau}} \equiv 1 - \frac{c_h}{y_h}$:

$$1-\overline{\overline{\tau}} \geq \frac{c_h}{y_h} \tag{4.37}$$

Note, that with a $\tau \leq \overline{\overline{\tau}}$, the debtor would either choose the efficient effort level at costs c_h, or abstain altogether if (4.38) does not hold. Note again, that it is also possible (and in fact for most parameters true) that $\overline{\tau} < \overline{\overline{\tau}}$, so that by meeting the incentive compatibility constraint the participation constraint will also hold.

The return to the creditor is $\tau n y_h$ and depends on the length of the period of good conduct, the garnishment rate and the difference across income levels. Hence it cannot be determined how the creditor's return compares to the current German regulation, i.e. $\tau n y_h \gtreqless m y_l$.

It should be noted that $\overline{\tau}$ and $\overline{\overline{\tau}}$ are highly dependent on the debtor's personal characteristics: her costs of effort, the differences in those cost levels, her income expectations, her possibilities of substitution (i.e. switching job) etc. It is, therefore, rather difficult to assess a garnishment rate, and much more so to asses a general τ. For practical purposes, it is most likely that a partial garnishment would fail to implement the first best effort.[14] Yet, a partial garnishment may be capable of mitigating the effects of the period of good conduct and providing the debtor with at some incentive to exert herself. A numeric example at the end of the ex-ante section provides some values, showing that the period of good conduct needs to be prolonged to ensure a comparable return to the creditor.

Still, even if the garnishment rate is too high, i.e. τ does not fulfill (4.35), the creditor may receive some compensation. The incentive structure is then similar to the current German regulation. It does not pay for the debtor to choose high effort during the period of good conduct, since she is neither compensated for her efforts by additional income, nor does it shorten the period of good conduct. Since according to the assumptions, abstention would be observable, the debtor would at least choose a low effort to not obviously violate the conditions of the period of good conduct. Hence, given that the consumer participates, she would at least choose a low effort during the period good conduct.

$$(T-n)(y_h - c_h) + n(1-\tau) y_l - nc_l \geq 0 \tag{4.38}$$

This means that the remaining income that rests with the consumer during the period of good conduct plus her expected income after the period of good conduct have to compensate her efforts. As a result, the returns to the participants, do not only depend τ as the rate of garnishment, but might moreover depend on the remaining periods after the period of good conduct. If (4.38) does not hold the consumer will refrain from any effort, consequentially bringing the creditor's return to zero.

Analogous to the German regulation, there is another possibility. If the outstanding debt is sufficiently small, the debtor will choose the efficient effort level. She will hope to repay the entire outstanding debt within the

[14] This objection gets more clear when the effort choice is thought of as a continuous parameter: for costs $c(e_i)$ with $e_i \in [e_l, e_h]$ and $\pi(e) \in [0,1]$, with $e' > 0$ and $e'' > 0$ and for $\pi : \pi'(e) > 0, \pi''(e) < 0$.
Here the incentive compatibility constraint for a continuos effort choice is the first order condition of the consumer's maximization problem giving $\tau = 1 - \frac{e'}{\pi' y}$. This condition to hold would require $\tau = 0$. However, an improvement in the debtor's incentives is possible, i.e. a higher effort as compared to the current German regulation might be chosen, and so the economic loss is reduced.

period of good conduct. This holds -irrespective of the rate of garnishment (τ)- if condition (4.9) holds. Still, this is not likely to happen, as outstanding debt must be rather small. In that case the debtor would usually attempt an out-of-court agreement with her creditors, which is less costly.

For the major parameters, the incentives for the debtor are not considerably altered and the results are similar to those under the current German regulation. A drawback of this regulation is that the creditors will have to wait longer to receive compensation, which becomes even more detrimental when interest is introduced.

To resume: with a partial garnishment for fixed period, depending on the relations of the parameters five different outcomes are possible:

(1) The garnishment rate τ is sufficiently small, $\tau \leq \bar{\bar{\tau}}$ and $\tau \leq \bar{\tau}$, the efficient effort level may be implemented, and the first best is achieved.
The garnishment rate is such that $\bar{\bar{\tau}} < \tau \leq \bar{\tau}$, but the consumer can be compensated by future income, i.e. (4.36) holds.

(2) The garnishment rate is sufficiently small, yet the participation constraint is not met. Hence the parameter combination is such that $\bar{\bar{\tau}} < \tau \leq \bar{\tau}$. The debtor will refrain from participation, and the return to both parties will be zero. Again, this result is marginal.

(3) The garnishment rate exceeds $\bar{\tau}$, but remaining debt D is sufficiently small so that the debtor will strive to pay it entirely during the period of good conduct. The efficient solution may be implemented, but would have also been implemented under the current German regulation or with no bankruptcy regulation at all.

(4) The garnishment rate exceeds $\bar{\tau}$ and the participation constraint holds. Here, the debtor will only choose a low effort during the period of good conduct, producing some return to the creditors.

(5) The garnishment rate exceeds $\bar{\tau}$ and the participation constraint fails to hold. The debtor will not participate in the regulation and consequentially the return is zero.

As noted, the last three cases were also observed in the German regulation. A statement about the likelihood of the various cases is rather difficult as statistical data is hardly available. However, it is reasonable to assume that, depending on the rate of garnishment, the first and the third case are the predominant cases.

Still, the second interpretation of the partial garnishment rule rests for the analysis. This is a variation of no debt release, instead of a 100% garnishment of the debtor's income in each period until the entire debt is paid off, $P = D$. Here, the garnishment rate is lowered to τ, and the debtor partially benefits from her endeavours.

Again I have to distinguish between several contingencies:

Similar to the partial garnishment for a fixed period, the debtor chooses a high effort, when she receives a strictly positive return in each period, $\tau \leq \overline{\overline{\tau}}$ and a higher return with the high effort level, $\tau \leq \overline{\tau}$. This ensures that the debtor gets a strictly positive return in each period, even if the unsettled debt exceeds $P^{\max}$. This corresponds to the first case of the partial garnishment rule for a fixed number of years. The creditor's full compensation depends on the garnishment rate τ and the remaining working time T, i.e. as long as $P \leq \tau T y_h$ the creditor will be fully compensated, otherwise he will receive at least some fraction $\tau T y_h$ of his claim.

Yet, even with a $\tau > \overline{\tau}$ the debtor might - depending on the amount of unsettled debt P - still choose the efficient effort level. This is similar to the analysis of no debt release. As long as she can expect a positive net return, she will choose the high effort level:

$$T\left(y_h - c_h\right) - P \geq 0 \tag{4.39}$$

or substitution $P = n\tau y_h$ gives

$$(1-\tau)\, n y_h + (T-n)\, y_h - T c_h \geq 0. \tag{4.40}$$

Note that for (4.40) to hold requires that P is paid in full. Otherwise the debtor could not expect a compensation for her efforts during the period of repayment. It also implies that the debtor will choose the high effort level. Since she will have to pay the entire amount, a fixed sum will be deducted from her income, in other words she is the residual claimant and will, hence, take the efficient decision. Yet, if (4.40) fails, the debtor will refrain from participation entirely. Note that the $P_\tau^{\max}$, derived for a partial garnishment rule, is considerably lower than the $P^{\max}$ deduced under no debt release.

To summarize: there are three possible outcomes

(1) The garnishment rate is sufficiently small, and the debtor receives a positive income in each period, i.e. $\tau \leq \overline{\overline{\tau}}$ and $\tau \leq \overline{\tau}$. The debtor

will choose the high effort level to avoid welfare loss.

(2) The garnishment rate exceeds $\overline{\tau}$, but the outstanding debt is sufficiently small, so that (4.40) holds.

(3) The garnishment rate exceeds $\overline{\tau}$, and (4.40) also does not hold. The debtor will abstain, giving a return of zero to both participants.

Only the first outcome, when $\tau \leq \overline{\overline{\tau}}$ and $P > P^{\max}$, the partial garnishment rule offers a welfare improvement in comparison to no debt release. There the debtor will choose the high effort level instead of abstention, thus generating at least some return to the creditor. However, compared to the no debt release rule in the other outcomes the partial garnishment either results in a lower compensation to the creditor, or incites the debtor to abstain at a lower amount of unsettled debt. Moreover, the assessment of the garnishment rate is highly dependent on the individual characteristics of the debtor. Her education, the possibility to alter effort decision (i.e. the difference between high and low effort), the working time left, etc. All these individual characteristics make it rather difficult to asses a rate τ that would provide the debtor with incentives to choose the efficient effort level. Yet, to ensure that the debtor has sufficient incentives to choose the efficient effort, she needs to be granted a rather large proportion of her return, leaving little compensation for the creditor. The numerical example at the end of this section provides some illustration of this. It suggests that the garnishment rate should not exceed 30%[15] and that the period of good conduct must be lengthened to about 10 years, in order to provide the creditor with similar compensation as the German regulation.

4.4.3 *Period of Supervision*

Many common law countries also employ a period of good conduct. However, the patterns of this period are quite different from the German period of good conduct. The debtor is not obliged to strive for payment of the outstanding claims, in order to increase the satisfaction rate of the creditors. Instead, the debtor is put under supervision by some authority who imposes various restrictions. For example, her ability to take new credit is greatly restricted, she may not act as an entrepreneur and even loses her passive voting right. This may seem, in the light of the present analysis,

[15] The present setup suggests an equal garnishment rate than the one instituted in Venice in 1195.

to be rather inefficient, as it hinders the debtor's economic activity while not producing return to the creditors. It follows from the previous analysis, that such obstacles hinder the debtor's economic activity rather than promoting it.

Again ex-post there is little benefit of this regulation, yet it does hold merits under a more broad consideration. Especially when taking the costs of garnishment and monitoring into account. Many defaulting debtors might have little or almost no expected income above subsistence level.[16] And monitoring the debtor's efforts during the period of good conduct would be quite costly for the court or the creditors themselves. Hence, there is little expected net surplus.

So instead of an attempt for costly recovery or as the opposite extreme an unconditional fresh start, the English regulation is taking a different way: imposing several obstacles on the debtor for a certain period, and thereby attempting to educate her towards a more careful treatment of credits.

This would create an ex-ante threat, as such a period of supervision would impose an inconvenience on the debtor. It gives a nonmalicious debtor an opportunity to become knowledgeable of the use of credit. Thus, such a regulation causes a sufficient ex-ante threat, while not seriously intervening with the debtor's working incentives.

Bankruptcy carries a social stigma, that a person who defaults on debt is considered to have done something evil. This social obligation to pay one's debts is found in many societies. Religion often compels their faithful to pay their debts by depicting the dreadful consequences of failure.[17] The English regulation fosters this stigma, in order to prevent debtors from careless credits.

Stigma also has a supportive ex-post role. The debtor experiences disutility from being governed during the period of good conduct, causing her to work harder to finish the period of good conduct as soon as possible. Under the proposed reform the presence of a stigma may further enhance the debtor's working incentives. Taking these non-monetary costs into ac-

[16] As an example, after the introduction of a consumer insolvency regulation many consumers were barred from the benefits of debt release as they were unable to afford the costs of the procedure. Accordingly a reform of the Insolvency Law came into effect on Dec. 1st 2001, allowing the debtor to apply for legal aid as well as a deferment of payment (see InsO § 4a-d and Fruhner 2002 for a discussion.)

[17] For example in the Hinduism, a faithful who fails to pay his debts is believed to be reborn in a lower caste (see Efrat 1998).

count, the consumer is - ceteris paribus - more willing to choose a high effort level in order to reduce the period of good conduct, i.e. the period that carries the bankruptcy stigma.

Let us assume that the consumer suffers a disutility d ($d > 0$) for each year of the period of good conduct. In order to be released from debt she has to pay the amount, P. The debtor can calculate that it takes n years with high and m years with low effort, to meet the payment obligation for debt release. In a prolonged period of good conduct, the accumulated disutility is $m \cdot d$, for the short period of good conduct it is $n \cdot d$. This affects the consumer's incentive compatibility in (4.4):

$$(T-n)\,y_h - nd - Tc_h \geq (T-m)\,(y_h - c_h) - md - mc_l \tag{4.41}$$

which can be rearranged to

$$\frac{m-n}{m}\,(y_h + d) \geq c_h - c_l. \tag{4.42}$$

Thus the gain from a shorter period of good conduct has to outmatch the additional costs of high effort. This incentive compatibility constraint is stricter than the one stated in (4.5), as the debtor enjoys additional income $(m-n)\,y_h$ that she weighs against the additional costs (left side of the inequality), and looses the stigma due to her efforts. Note, that when the period of good conduct is of fixed length, the presence of stigma does not enhance the debtor's incentives, since she is not able to alter the length of the period.

To resume: Several obstacles placed on the debtor during the period of good conduct enhance the ex-ante threat of bankruptcy, and foster the debtor's efforts during the period of good conduct. Since the consumer suffers from being governed she is c.p. more interested in reducing the period of bankruptcy and thus interested in exerting more effort. A period of supervision can be beneficial if there are considerable costs of wage garnishment and supervision during the period of good conduct, and the defaulting debtor has no considerable future non-exempt income. Instead of costly garnishment this law imposes a non-monetary disutility on the debtor, thereby teaching her from her previous failure.

4.5 Return to the Creditor

So far the analysis has focused on the debtor's decision problem, as posed by the various regulations, particularly her incentives to create working income. As explained, this is the predominant concern of the ex-post analysis. Although, the return to the creditors ex-post does not concern welfare, their satisfaction rate is vital in a broader context. The overall effects of the debt release regulation depend on how much compensation the creditor may expect. Hence, the return to the creditor under the various regulations is summarized below.

- *Chapter 7*
  This regulation grants an immediate fresh start to the debtor. The creditor will receive no return aside from the revenue due to seizure of the debtor's assets. Yet, the value of the assets is assumed to be zero, he receives no return at all.
  In short $P = A = 0$.
- *No debt release*
  When the bankruptcy regulation does not provide a procedure for debt release, the debtor is obliged to repay all unsettled debt, regardless of the circumstances. Yet, it is shown that the debtor will do so, only to a certain threshold. As a result the creditor is either fully satisfied or receives nothing at all,
  i.e. $P = \begin{cases} D, & \text{if } D \leq P^{\max} \\ 0, & \text{if } D > P^{\max} \end{cases}$
- *German Regulation*
  The German regulation (1999) grants debt release to the honest debtor, while still promising compensation for six years of income plus the debtor's entire non-exempt assets. Yet, the analysis shows that the regulation provides insufficient incentives to the debtor during the period of good conduct. Hence, the returns to the creditor are the result of mediocre effort,
  i.e. $P = A + 6y_l$.
- *Chapter 13*
  Under U.S. Chapter 13 the debtor compensates the creditor with three years income. Note, that Chapter 13 is seldom chosen. However, the incentives to the debtor are similar to those of the German regulation, hence, she only choose a mediocre effort,

i.e. $P = 3y_l$.

- *Proposal*
  Under the proposed reform the creditor may expect to receive amount P equal either to the entire debt or some maximum amount set according to the debtor's abilities,
  i.e. $P = \max\{D, P^{\max}\}$.
- *Variable period of good conduct*
  With a variable period of good conduct the debtor's incentives are improved compared to the current German regulation. Thus the expected compensation of the creditor is:
  $P = A + (m - r)\, y_h$.
- *Partial Garnishment*
  As the analysis has shown the effect of a partial garnishment rule is highly dependent on several variables including the actual garnishment rate, the debtor's personal characteristics, her remaining working time, the difference between high and low effort etc. Thus, a general statement of the effects of the regulation on the return given to the creditor is difficult to assess.
- *Stigma and other non-monetary penalties*
  A period of education does not create any return to the creditor per se, nor does the existence of a social stigma. Yet, these measures cause the debtor to be more cautious ex-ante, and may encourage the debtor to fulfill the requirements for debt release quickly.

The results are summarized in Figure 4.4 below.

4.6 Numerical Example

A numerical example may provide some clarification of the results if the previously conducted analysis. The average gross labor income in Germany amounts to approximately Euro 27,000 a year. Assuming a subsistence level of Euro 10,000 per year, the disposable net working income amounts to Euro 17,000, i.e. $y_1 = 17,000$. According to the German regulation the period of good conduct lasts six years. The time horizon, e.g. to receive labor income, is set to $T = 15$, may be regarding a 50 years old person who expects to work until the age of 65. Spending a high effort, the consumer will earn $y_1 = 17,000$ with probability $\pi_h = 0.9$, and with probability

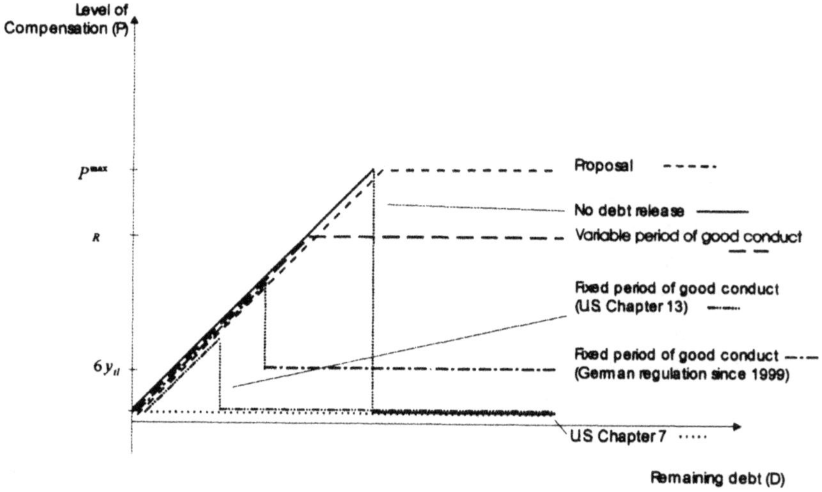

Fig. 4.4 Compensation of the creditor under the various regulations.

$(1-\pi_h)$ her disposable income will be $y_2 = 5,000$. The expected income of $y_h = 15,800$. With low effort the probability for the high realization is only $\pi_l = 0.4$, resulting in an expected income of $y_l = 9,800$. The costs of effort to create disposable income are assumed to be $c_h = 6,000 > c_l = 4,000$. The remaining debt after seizure of the assets amounts to $D = 150,000$, i.e. about four times the gross labor income. The debtor is assumed to have no seizable assets, $A = 0$. Note, that without any debt release, the debtor would abstain from any effort at all, i.e. $D \geq P^{max}$ or $150,000 > 15 \cdot (15,800 - 6,000) = 147,000$. The consumer would not be willing to pay back the debt, though she would be well capable of accumulating sufficient money in her remaining working time, $15 \cdot 15,800 = 237,000$. The return resulting with the various regulations is stated below:

- With *Chapter 7* the creditor would only have the right to seize the debtor's assets. His return would be zero, while the debtor faces an unconstraint maximization of future income. Thus her expected working income is $Y_D = T \cdot y_h = 15 \cdot (15,800 - 6,000) = 147,000$.
- In the case of *no debt release* regulation, the debtor would refuse any attempt of repayment, for the unsettled debt exceeds her maximum willingness to pay, $P > P^{max}$. Hence, the return to the creditor and the debtor's expected future income is zero.

- With *a fixed period of good conduct,* as the German regulation, and Chapter 13, the debtor has only mediocre incentives to work. The return to the creditor under German regulation: $P = A + 6y_l = 0 + 6 \cdot 9{,}800 = 58{,}800$. And the debtor could expect an income of $Y_D = (T-6)(y_h - c_h) - 6c_l = 64{,}200$.
  With Chapter 13 the return is similar, yet the length of the period of good conduct is 3 instead of 6 years, $P = 3y_l = 29{,}400$ and the debtor receives an income of $Y_D = 105{,}600$.
- If the period of good conduct is of variable length, as proposed by Bigus & Steiger (2002), the creditor could still expect a similar amount as the current German regulation, while the debtor would be provided with better incentives. The expected return to the creditor is similar to the German regulation, $P = 58{,}800$. Yet, the debtor has the choice to strive for an abbreviated period of 3.72 years, or to endure the full length of six years (as $m - r = P/y_h = 3.72$). $P = my_l = 6 \cdot 0.5 \cdot 9{,}800 = (m-r)\,y_h = 3.72 \cdot 15{,}800 = 58{,}800$. Expected income with high effort amounts to $Y_S - P = 88{,}200$.
  To justify this reform the intertemporal effects are considered: Assume that the consumer adjusts her effort level at the beginning of each period. Given that she receives a low return in the first year, the maximum remaining length of good conduct is 5 years, with a remaining payment of 49,000, abbreviated length $m_t - r_t = P/y_h = 3.4$ years. To see whether she would still choose the high effort I check with formula (4.32) $r_t \geq [m_t (c_h - c_l)]/y_h = [5 \cdot (6{,}000 - 4{,}000)]/15{,}800 \approx 0.633$. Thus, she would still participate with a high effort. The same is true if also the return in the second year is low. She would then choose a low effort for the remaining time of the period of good conduct, only when the return for the third consecutive year is low. Note, that this event is unlikely as it appears only with the probability $(1-\pi_h)^3 = 0.001$.
  Similar calculations may be done when the variable period of good conduct is compared to Chapter 13 with a period 3 or 5 years.
- When the partial garnishment rule is employed, the return to the creditor depends on the length of the period of good conduct as well as the garnishment rate. To ensure a high effort during the period of good conduct the garnishment rate could be at most $\overline{\tau} \leq 1 - ((c_h - c_l)/(y_h - y_l)) = 0.\overline{3}$ according to (4.35). Ergo, the

period of good conduct - to provide the creditor with a compensation rate similar to the German regulation - would have to be prolonged to 11.2 years. Yet, in this case no welfare loss would occur, as the consumer would choose the efficient effort level. With a higher garnishment rate, the debtor would choose the low effort during the period of good conduct, consequently the period of good conduct would have to be considerably prolonged, and no welfare improvement could be made.

- Finally, with the *proposal,* the debtor would be asked for the maximum amount $P^{max} = 147,000$. This would capture all of the debtor's expected surplus. The debtor could expect to fulfill the requirement within 9.3 years. Yet, when considering intertemporal effects, such an amount does not seem to be wise. For instance, if her realization in the first period after bankruptcy ($t = 3$) is low, the remaining payment $P_t = 142,000$ would be more than her net expected income $Y_D = 14 \cdot y_h - c_h = 137,200$. Consequently, she would cease to participate. Thus the debtor should be given some surplus, to insure participation in later periods. So if the debtor would be required to pay $P = 100,000$, she has an expected length of the payment period of 6.32 years. In case of low realization, she would cease to participate only after a low realization of nine consecutive years. However, this is quite unlikely, with a probability of $(1 - \pi_h)^9 = 0.000000001$. Hence, the proposal offers the highest return of all possible regulations to the creditor, while not distorting the debtor's working incentives.

4.7 Discussion

The ex-post analysis has produced several results, this section discusses the assumptions and gives implications of these results.

Effort level

The findings are based on the assumption that the individual's effort level is not observable. It is possible to detect effort via monitoring.[18] Yet, this would normally incur high costs on the monitoring authority, which would,

[18] For instance, the local court in Hamburg dismissed a debtor from his period of good conduct because he only had a part time job, which the court found to be an insufficient effort.(see AG Hamburg 20.Nov. 2000 Az: 68e IK 15/99)

moreover, be inefficient. Instead, the proposed reform offers a regulation in which it is in the debtor's interest to fulfill the required payment as quickly as possible rendering any monitoring effort futile. The assumption of a discrete effort level is made for simplicity. A continuos effort level does not change the results of the analysis. A fixed amount, as a requirement for debt release, does not change the debtor's first order condition - on which she bases her effort level decision. Also, the assumption that abstention is observable may be relaxed, and would result in an even lower return to the creditors for the German regulation. Yet, the fact that the debtor cannot be forced to strive for payment of outstanding debt is well established by experience, and it was in fact in many European countries the main motivation to introduce debt release regulation. Another objection might be the consumer's ability to alter her effort level. Once, someone has found employment it is difficult to reduce working hours, making the action easily observed. Yet, the individual may become less devoted to her job, thereby increasing the probability of being dismissed. Still, a bankrupt individual is often unemployed, and the efforts to find a job can easily be adjusted by the individual.

Restrictions for practical use

The paper proposes regulation that sets a specific amount as a prerequisite for debt release that is contingent on the unsettled debt and the individual debtor's abilities (i.e. her income expectations). To be of practical relevance, a regulation should require as little information as possible from the governing authorities. Though, the assessment of future income comprises certain difficulties, a reasonable prediction should be possible. Moreover, it requires less information than, for example, the estimation of a garnishment rate that would leave the debtor's effort decision undistorted. Yet, it might be advisable, to set a maximum length of the period of good conduct, in order to prevent an unsought prolongation that may result from low income realizations. It was shown that such a truncation of the period of good conduct may cause the debtor to lower her effort and 'wait' for the period of good conduct to pass in later periods. Yet, this would only happen in marginal cases. Another problem might be the fact that some debtors do not have an expected income worth mentioning. Yet, the question whether these debtors should be obliged to pay nothing and consequentially get an immediate fresh start, or be obliged to endure a period of supervision similar to the English regulation, is not answered with the analysis done so far. This has consequences for the ex-ante incentives, which are dealt with

in the next section. From a pure ex-post perspective, these debtors should receive an immediate debt release. Any other regulation is likely to distort incentives or incur unwarranted costs on the governing authority. The costs of the bankruptcy procedure were not accounted for in the model. The effects of these costs may be relevant but are beyond the scope of the present analysis and are therefore left for future research.
In fact the Canadian bankruptcy regulation contains some interesting features, which meet the requirements postulated in this analysis. Here, under certain circumstances the debtor may file a 'consumer proposal' where she suggests to pay a portion of the outstanding claims over the next 3-5 years. Debt discharge is contingent on the completion of the plan (see McGregor, Klingander and Lown (2001)). Yet, the amount agreed to be paid back an be adjusted (higher or lower) if there are changes in the bankrupt's circumstances. This may on the one hand be understood as a hardship discharge to prevent an undue prolongation as discussed in the inter-temporal section. On the other hand this may destroy the debtor's economic incentive to exert herself and increase her income. The model suggests that an adjustment is not advisable, instead a maximal length may be instituted. Yet, the Canadian regulation shows that it is well possible to estimate the expected income.
It might be argued that a debt release regulation contingent on the debtor's abilities is unfair, as it taxes the debtor's against her level of education. Yet, the debtor's application for credit was also assessed according to her abilities, hence, her education. Finally, for simplicity the prospects of illicit work or hidden income are not considered.

Contractual solutions and out of court renegotiations

The model does not consider out-of-court negotiations. Yet, these are of course possible and desirable, as it would most likely save transaction costs. In any case a bankruptcy regulation provides a disagreement or threat point in renegotiations. This is desirable as the bargaining power (in the absence of a bankruptcy regulation) is often in favour of the creditor. For example, under the rather debtor friendly regulation of the U.S. it is observed that creditors are much more willing to renegotiate the terms of the contract than in Germany.

Simplifying assumptions

The model contains a number of simplifying assumptions, made solely for convenience, which may be relaxed without altering the results. The interest rate was set to zero. Yet, since it is in the interest of the debtor to pay the obligated sum as soon as possible, she will minimize the loss of interest that the creditor endures. Also income realizations were assumed to be fixed and independent of each other. Relaxing these assumptions would greatly complicate the analysis without producing more meaningful results. Therefore, these assumptions are kept.

The fixed period of good conduct

In the German regulation the debtor is obliged to attempt to repay during the succeeding six years. The analysis showed that this fixed period leaves the debtor with no incentives to perform well. Even though the opposite had clearly been in the intention of the law maker; the debtor should try hard and show remorse during that period, which is further established by the fact that debt release is only granted at the end of the period, if the court finds her to be sufficiently qualified. This means high effort is desired by the lawmaker, yet there is no direct reward for the individual. It should be noted that even the German regulation provides some incentive mechanisms for the debtor. For example heritages received during the period of good conduct are only garnished with 50%. Also her income is not entirely garnished during the whole period of good conduct, during the fifth and sixth year 10%, 20% resp. of her income are being redistributed to the debtor by the trustee, - the garnishment rate is diminished (§292 InsO).

Optimal Regulation

The analysis did not strive to find the optimal regulation, rather it evaluated several existing regulations and scholarly proposals and suggested a reform that outmatches all existing regulations. It is shown that the proposed regulation may lead to distortions in the debtor's incentives, yet these effects are rather marginal. Finding an optimal regulation - given that it exists at all - has proven to be complicated and highly dependent on the debtor's characteristics. Instead, the proposed regulation suggests a determined amount, which is within the debtor's ability to pay. This is a rather simple mechanism that implements the optimal solution for the majority of the parameters.

Statistical evaluation

The paper does not provide statistical support for its findings. Yet, such data is hardly available in most European countries, for example the German regulation was enacted only in 1999 and thus far no one has yet accomplished the period of good conduct. Moreover, in most European countries statistical data on consumer bankruptcy is elusive. Also, in this paper various regulations and proposals from different jurisdictions are evaluated.

Such a comparison would require an additional paper. Undoubtedly, the availability of some data would strengthen the results. This is an area left for future research.

4.8 Results and Implications

It has been shown that a bankruptcy regulation does not only affect credit contracts and the incentives of the parties in such contracts, but also has considerable effects on the debtor's choices post filing. And some regulations create serious distortions, resulting in welfare losses that harm both parties. To create an improved regulation the boundedness of the debtor's ability and willingness to pay needs to be taken into consideration. Undoubtedly, Chapter 7 is the cheapest and fasted way for the creditor to gain some returns, and it will never distort the debtor's economic performance ex-post. From a pure welfare ex-post perspective Chapter 7 seems to be the best outcome. Yet, it was shown to be possible to enhance the creditor's position while maintaining the debtor's incentives. Further results produced by the analysis thus far, are restated below.

(1) *Chapter 7* causes the least distortions as the debtor will always choose the efficient effort ex-post. However, the creditor is left insufficiently satisfied.
(2) Generally, *no debt release* will not set the best ex-post incentives for the debtor, but there is a maximal amount the debtor can be asked for, i.e. some form of debt discharge is ex-post efficient.
(3) A fixed *period of good conduct* sets insufficient incentives for the debtor to work hard.
(4) The *proposal* suggested that a particular amount set as precondition for debt release, generates better incentives for the debtor to choose a high effort. Note, that this amount depends on her individual situation and skills.
(5) Due to the debtor's limited wealth, it is not advisable to deprive her of the entire expected surplus, doing so may result in the debtor's abstention in later periods. Hence, she cannot be brought down to her reservation utility and will receive some surplus.
(6) Under the proposed rule the debtor is still willing to work hard, even if she is risk averse.

(7) The existence of a collateral or its value has no effect on the individual's effort choice ex-post. Similarly the assignment of the collateral to a particular party has no welfare effects ex-post.

(8) Comparing the regulations with respect to the creditor's collection rate, the proposal regulation generally outperforms all other aforementioned regulations.

Chapter 5
Ex-Ante Analysis

Previously, the analysis focused the effects of various bankruptcy regulations on debtor's incentives to work after filing. Most existing regulation entail a welfare loss ex-post, as they provoke the debtor to choose an insufficient effort, sometimes even resulting in the abstention from any economic activity. A rule was proposed to circumvent such welfare losses. Yet, the analysis has also shown that from an ex-post perspective debt release remains an inevitable quality of a bankruptcy code. Taking the necessity for debt release for granted, this chapter investigates whether the prospect of debt release accounts for changes in the credit contracts and how this converts the choices of the participants. Since the bankruptcy regulation determines the case of default, it, thereby partly, sets the provisions of a credit contract, and thus establishes the participants' incentives. In particular, such regulation influence the debtor's motivation to pay debts. It is often postulated that the prospect of debt release distorts the debtor's endeavors to repay her credit so that the bankruptcy provisions affect the costs and availability of credit adversely.[1] The logic is as follows: since under some regulations the debtor does not have to pay the entire debt in all states, she might be tempted to maliciously default or at least to choose an insufficient effort. This may result in credits becoming less available or too costly for consumers, thereby causing a welfare loss. In a hidden action model it is investigated if and how much the discussed regulations distort the debtor's ex-ante choices.

The chapter is organized as follows: section 5.1 introduces the addi-

[1] see e.g. White (1998), Jacoby (2002), Hynes and Posner (2002).

tional assumptions and in the following section the first-best solution is stated as a benchmark. In the succeeding section, the effects of the four conventionalized bankruptcy rules are discussed, followed by a discussion of the effects of several potential extensions, such as the existence of a collateral and the moral connotations of bankruptcy. Then in section 5.5 a quantification of these effects is given. Finally, section 5.6 examines the effects of the debtor's risk attitude, first by relying on classic risk aversion and then by investigating possible behavior of a bounded rational debtor. The chapter closes with a discussion of the results, their implications and limits of the findings.

5.1 Setting

In accordance to the time structure, as introduced in Figure 3.1 and further elaborated in Figure 5.1, I focus now on the dates $t = -2$ to $t = 0$: i.e. how the debtor's effort decision - which influences the likelihood of the shock - is affected by the patterns of the bankruptcy code.

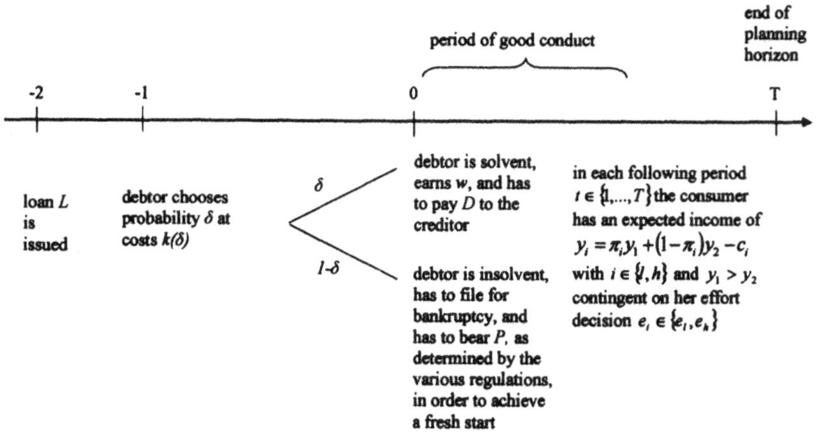

Fig. 5.1 Time structure ex-ante

For this part of the analysis these additional assumptions are made

- The debtor borrowed a credit or loan L at $t = -2$ from the creditor, which she uses to buy some asset A. The loan provides some benefit to the debtor where Λ is the monetary equivalent of the benefit.[2] The loan is due at $t = 0$ with a payment of D.
- Meanwhile, at $t = 1$, in order to meet her debt obligation, the debtor has to acquire some wealth w , with $w \geq D$.[3] This wealth is subject to a random shock: with probability δ, $\delta \in [0,1]$, the debtor is fortunate and earns w. With probability $(1-\delta)$ her endeavors do not prove fruitful, she earns nothing and she must file for bankruptcy. The realization of income is assumed to be observable and verifiable, i.e. the debtor cannot hide w and pretend to be insolvent

$$\tilde{w} = \begin{cases} w, & \text{with prob. } \delta \\ 0, & \text{with prob. } (1-\delta)\,. \end{cases} \tag{5.1}$$

- In the solvent state she has to pay the creditor D. When being bankrupt, she has to endure the reprisals of the applicable bankruptcy regulation and pays P out of her future income.
- The debtor may influence the probability of realizing each state by choosing some effort at cost k. For simplicity, the parameters are set so that the debtor may choose the probability δ at costs $k(\delta)$ with $k' > 0, k'' > 0$. The cost function is strictly increasing in δ and has, furthermore, the following properties $k(0) = 0$ and $k(1) = \infty$. This means that an investment of zero would cause a definite default, while a 100% reduction in the probability of default is infinitely costly.
- As introduced in section 3. and analyzed 4. the debtor has a working income of y_t during each period $t \geq 1$. In this section only the accumulated income needs to be considered. Y_S indicates accumulated expected net future income after $t = 2$, with $t \in \{1, ..., T\}$, in the solvent and Y_B accumulated future income in the insolvent

[2] To keep things simple, the debtor is assumed to derive the entire benefit of this asset immediately, and afterwards the asset has no use for her nor any considerable resale value, e.g. the debtor uses the loan to finance a fancy vacation trip.

[3] One might also think of w as the income of several periods as L might be rather large, and it takes the debtor in case of distress several periods to pay P.

(bankrupt) state, with $Y_{S/B} = T(y_i - c_i)$, with $i \in \{l, h\}$ as introduced in section 3.1.[4] For the time being, future income expectations, i.e. income after $t = 2$, are assumed to remain unchanged due to bankruptcy. Yet, the debtor's effort choices may be altered due to the provisions of the bankruptcy code, making her income expectations also dynamic. To indicate these changes the index Y_B is used as an example: Under the 'no debt release' regulation when $D > P^{\max}$ the debtor abstains ($Y_B = 0$), making the return to both parties is zero. For example, when the bankruptcy regulation causes no distortions, as for example under Chapter 7, $Y_B = Y_S$. The purpose of this assumption is to separate the various effects, changes in income expectations due to distress will be discussed later in this chapter.

- The debtor has no other monetary worth that could be seized upon filing, in particular, the asset purchased at $t = -2$ with the credit has no resale value at $t = 0$.
- Participants are again assumed to be risk neutral, and the discount rate remains zero, for the time being.
- The credit market is perfectly competitive, creditors make an expected profit of zero.

Having set those additional assumptions, I now determine the conditions that shape the participant's incentives. The debtor chooses δ in order to maximize her future income:

$$\max_{\delta} \Lambda + \delta (w - D + Y_S) + (1 - \delta)(Y_B - P) - k(\delta). \tag{5.2}$$

The debtor's income consists of the benefit derived from the loan Λ plus her future income. In the solvent state she earns w and pays D to the creditor and has furthermore a future income of Y_S. In the insolvent state the debtors return in $t = -1$ is zero, while she has to pay P from her future income Y_B.

It is assumed that at $t = -2$ borrowing is beneficial for the debtor, since it increased her expected utility, i.e. $U_C \geq U_{NC}$, with the index C and NC

[4] When the debtor is solvent, she will choose the efficient effort e_h in each following period. When she is insolvent, her effort decision is subject to the provisions of the applicable bakruptcy code, as it was discussed in the ex-post analysis.

representing the utility with a credit and no credit respectively

$$\begin{aligned} U_C &\geq U_{NC} \Rightarrow \\ & \Lambda + \delta (w - D + Y_S) + (1 - \delta)(Y_B - P) - k(\delta) \\ &\geq \delta (w + Y_S) + (1 - \delta) Y_B - k(\delta). \end{aligned} \tag{5.3}$$

While the creditor, as he is acting within a competitive market, may only insure an expected profit of zero

$$\delta D + (1 - \delta) P - L = 0. \tag{5.4}$$

As follows, the additional condition for insolvency out to be set that the payment in the bad state cannot exceed the one in the good state

$$D \geq L \geq P \geq 0. \tag{5.5}$$

P -or more precisely an upper bound for P- is determined by the applicable bankruptcy regime. Hence, the creditor's only latitude is to adjust D so that (5.4) holds. Thus, these three decisions are taken simultaneously when signing the credit contract. At time $t = -1$, the debtor decides on both the effort level or whether and not to take the credit. Likewise, the creditor chooses D also at time $t = -1$.

5.2 First Best

The social optimum is found by jointly maximizing the returns of both participants $Y_D + Y_C$ i.e. (5.2) + (5.4). Additionally, at the first-best the debtor's ex-post choices are not distorted, $Y_S = Y_B$.

$$\max_{\delta} \Lambda - L + Y_S + \delta w - k(\delta) \tag{5.6}$$

which when being maximized yields:

$$w = k'(\delta^*). \tag{5.7}$$

Solving for δ, equation (5.7) determines δ^* to be the debtor's first best effort level. Due to the patterns of the cost function which is strictly increasing in δ, it can be said that the higher the right hand side of (5.7) the higher selected δ will be. Hence, a non-distorting bankruptcy regime should insure that the debtor chooses an effort level such that its costs are $k(\delta^*)$. Equation (5.7) states that the debtor should choose δ such that marginal costs should equal the marginal return in $t = -1$, i.e. her decision should only be determined by the return created in that period. Since future income is, by assumption, not affected by the effort level chosen in $t = -1$. Note, that this outcome is equivalent to the debtor's effort decision with no credit. This is not a coincidence - the credit is not used for production or to alter the debtor's income expectations, hence, it will not change her effort decision. If a regulation does change the debtor's decision, particularly if she lowers her precaution due to debt release, adverse consequences, such as increased risk premium or credit rationing will occur. The following chapter analyzes how the debtor performs under the various regulations, and what likely consequences this may have on the credit contract.

5.3 Performance of Various Rules

The ex-post analysis focuses on both the incentives generated by bankruptcy regulation for the debtor to work post-filing as well as the resulting returns. This part investigates how ex-post consequences of the various regimes affect the ex-ante situation: namely the availability of credits, the charged risk premium and, most important, the debtor's effort decision at $t = -1$ that determines the default probability.

In contrast to the first-best, participants make their choices simultaneously and independently. This is analyzed by first determining the factors which settle the debtor's choices and then considering the adjustments made by the creditor.
The debtor faces the maximization problem as stated in (5.2), which leads to the following first order condition:

$$w - D + P + Y_S - Y_B = k'(\delta). \tag{5.8}$$

Solved for δ (5.8) determines the default probability that the debtor chooses. Remember, her cost are strictly increasing in δ, i.e. the more precaution she takes against distress the more it costs her. The debtor's decision rests entirely on the difference in income realization in correspondence to her costs. All positive elements in (5.8) increase her return from being solvent and consequently incite her to choose a higher δ, while the negative elements have the opposite effects. As opposed to the situation without credit her choice depends now on both the immediate return w created in $t = -1$, on the credit payment in each state and the changes in income expectations caused by insolvency. As a result, (5.8) will only correspond to (5.7), i.e. implement the first-best effort choice, in a limited number of cases: either when $Y_S = Y_B$ and $D = P$, or, more generally, when $P - D + Y_S - Y_B = 0$. If this holds, the regulations of the bankruptcy regime implement the first best δ^*. In all other cases, a different δ will be chosen by the debtor, and -as to be shown in the analysis- a lower δ ($\delta < \delta^*$) is most likely.

Analyzing (5.8) shows that the benefit from the loan (Λ) is not relevant to the debtor's effort decision. This is because Λ is assumed to last for only for one period and the debtor will fully enjoy it regardless of her wealth at $t = 0$ (i.e. whether she is solvent). Yet, the benefit that was relevant when the debtor decided on the loan L, as Λ must have been sufficiently large in order to ensure her participation (see (5.3)). Therefore, only the costs of effort $k(\delta)$ and the difference across credit payments $(D - P)$ are relevant to her choice of δ at $t = -1$. In the good state she receives a considerably lower proportion, $w - D$, of her endeavours, while in the bad state she will pay less than or equal to the amount in the good state $(P \leq D)$.

Yet, in the analysis the decision at $t = -1$ has consequences beyond the immediate income realization, w. It may affect her future wealth, particularly when her future effort decision is distorted by the patterns of the bankruptcy regulation, i.e. $Y_B \neq Y_S$.

From an investigation of the general consequences of debt release on the debtor's decision, it transpires that the prospect of debt release most likely decreases the δ selected by the debtor, $\delta^* > \delta$. As the bankruptcy code determines an upper bound for the payment in case of distress (P), the relation $P \leq L \leq D$ was set in (5.5). When there is no debt release, i.e. $P = D$, and post bankruptcy income remains unchanged, the loan causes no deviations from δ^*.[5]

Otherwise, when $P < D$ the bankruptcy regulation determines an upper bound in case that distortions in P may arise. Since the debtor has to pay less in case of distress, her return in the bad state increases and the

5 Except for the case when $P > P^{max}$, which will be analyzed in detail under the regulation no debt release.

two payments no longer cancel each other out, i.e. the reduced income $(w - D)$ in the solvent state is no longer balanced by a similar payment of P in the insolvent state. Furthermore, the creditor needs to increase D to maintain his participation constraint (see (5.4)). This further reduces the debtor's incentives to remain solvent. In short, a higher D results in a lower remaining good-state return $(w - D)$ for the debtor. Consequently, the debtor's choice of δ will also be lower. The debtor's adjustment may be found by substituting the creditor's reaction function (5.4) into the debtor's first order condition (5.8):

$$w - \frac{L - P}{\delta} + Y_S - Y_B = k'(\delta). \tag{5.9}$$

Which solved for δ determines the default probability δ^c chosen by the debtor in a particular credit contract. The creditor adjusts D so that δ^c is stable for a given L and P. It may be seen that the lower the payment in the insolvent state, the more the creditor has to increase D in order to ensure his participation. This in turn provokes the debtor to further lower her effort as she benefits less from effort.

Future income may be affected by the provisions of bankruptcy regulation, $Y_B \leq Y_S$. The equation (5.8) states that the larger the possible loss due to bankruptcy, the greater the precaution the debtor will take. Yet, as shown in the ex-post analysis, a lowered income due to the bankruptcy provisions involves a welfare loss. This has several consequences: First the decrease in future income results only from adjustments of the debtor's effort decision, and these adjustments would hardly be to her own detriment. Hence, reductions in income expectations due to distress are always carried out at the expense of the creditor, i.e. any reduction in Y_B reduces P to the same extent. Yet, this reduction affects the debtor in additional two ways. The creditor, in anticipation of this effect, will increase D to maintain his zero profit constraint (5.4). This reduces the debtor's return from the good state and lowers her δ. The second effect incites the debtor to increase ex-ante precaution. Though, the debtor now saves on the cost of creating income post bankruptcy (as she reduces her effort or abstains completely), she forgoes this potential income due to insolvency. The second effect is likely to outweigh the first effect so long that Y_S is sufficiently large, yet the δ chosen will never exceed δ^* which becomes clear when discussing the effects of the no debt release regulation in more detail. The interplay of these two effects will be explored in the numerical example.

To resume: Several factors influence the debtor's ex-ante decision. Besides the wealth w generated at $t = -1$, the difference across the credit payments $(D-P)$ and the potential changes in income expectations created by the bankruptcy regulation also determine the debtor's decision. One general conclusion may be drawn:

Proposition 5.1 *Any form of debt release causes a risk-neutral debtor to lower her efforts ex-ante to avoid bankruptcy below the first best, $\delta < \delta^*$.*

The following paragraph details the effects of each stylized bankruptcy regime.

5.3.1 *Chapter 7*

When a debtor files for bankruptcy under U.S. Chapter 7, the creditor can seize current non-exempt assets, but has no claim on future income. As a result, the debtor's effort decision *ex-post* is not distorted, i.e. $Y_S = Y_B$. Since in this setting, the debtor was assumed to have no further belongings, the expected collection rate of the creditor in the insolvent state is zero, i.e. $P = A = 0$. This means the creditor increases D considerably to ensure at least an expected profit of zero, so that $L = \delta D$. The debtor chooses her effort according to

$$w - D = k'(\delta). \tag{5.10}$$

Compared to (5.7), it may be seen that this rule only diminishes the debtor's return at $t = -1$ while having no adverse consequences on her future income in case of distress. Hence, this rule gives the debtor little incentive to raise her precaution against insolvency. As a result, Ch. 7 creates the largest ex-ante distortions of all discussed regulations. This effect may be mitigated through a larger income, w, enabling the debtor to keep more wealth in the solvent state. Another possibility is the existence of non-exempt property which increases both the debtor's incentives to take precaution and the creditor's collection rate.[6] The effects of seizable as-

[6] For a discussion of the effects of collaterals and the effects of personal appreciation of a collateral in reaffirmations, see Adler et al. (2000).

sets are briefly discussed in the following section when considering possible extensions.

5.3.2 *No Debt Release*

No debt release is the other extreme - the debtor has unlimited liability for the debts, with her entire current and future belongings. The ex-post analysis shows that the debtor is willing to strive for payment of this outstanding debt so long as the required payment does not exceed $P^{\max}$. Two cases need to be differentiate between :

- $P \leq P^{\max}$ and
- $P > P^{\max}$.

For the former ($P \leq P^{\max}$), the analysis is relatively straight forward: The creditor always receives the entire outstanding debt and has no need to charge a risk premium, i.e. $L = D = P$. In the debtor's first order condition (5.8) the additional terms cancel out, and the condition is equivalent to the first-best (5.7). She will choose the efficient δ^*. Therefore, no debt release supports the efficient allocation within this range.

The latter case ($P > P^{\max}$) is different. As the ex-post analysis has shown, the regulation involves a welfare loss. The remaining debt exceeds the debtor's expected working income in case of distress. As a result, the debtor prescinds from any effort, and her expected future income is $Y_B = 0$. This, in turn, causes the recovery rate of the creditor to drop to zero ($P = Y_B = 0$). Even though, the creditor's ex-ante expected collection rate in case of distress is equivalent to the one of Chapter 7, i.e. zero, the ex-ante incentive effect to the debtor is not. By defaulting, she loses her entire potential future income, or, more precisely, any further endeavors are made futile. Her ex-ante effort decision is thus determined by:

$$w - D + Y_S = k'(\delta). \tag{5.11}$$

$D = \frac{L}{\delta}$ is the payment to the creditor in the good state, and is determined in a similar way as under Ch. 7, by the creditor's zero profit constraint (5.4). Yet, here the debtor will choose a significantly higher δ, since she looses Y_S when being insolvent. Nonetheless, it should be noted that in the present setup the δ chosen never exceeds δ^*, since the future income is always smaller than the debt payment, $Y_S \leq D$. This becomes clear when considering that future income expectations are assumed to remain unchanged during distress so long as the bankruptcy regime is non-distorting, i.e. $Y_S = Y_B$. Hence, since $P > P^{\max}$, even in the solvent state her future income would be insufficient to pay the debts, $D = P > Y_{S/B} = P^{\max}$. As a consequence, the debtor will have to increase the risk premium so that w has to be rather large to pay the credit. And the smaller Y_S is the smaller the precaution the debtor will take is. This situation is likely to occur when the debtor has only a few working periods.

5.3.3 *German Regulation*

Under the current German insolvency regulation, the debtor's liability is bounded to her assets and income during the period of good conduct. In terms of the model $P = 6y_l + A$, this regulation involves welfare loss ex-post. Therefore, I must distinguish between the return to the creditor and the effects on the debtor.

The creditor may expect some compensation even when the debtor is in distress. Due to the distorting effects of this regulation ex-post, the debtor's income differs across the provisions of various codes: $Y_S = T\,(y_h - c_h)$ and $Y_B = (T-6)\,(y_h - c_h) - 6c_l$. Therefore, her effort decision is now based on

$$w - D + 6\,(y_h - c_h - c_l) = k'\,(\delta) \tag{5.12}$$

substituting the creditor's reaction function (5.4) gives:

$$w - \frac{L}{\delta} + \frac{1-\delta}{\delta} 6y_l + 6\,(y_h - c_h + c_l) = k'\,(\delta)\,. \tag{5.13}$$

The distorting effect of the regulation is captured in (5.13) that the return to the creditor and the effect on the debtor fall apart. The debtor looses in case of distress is constituted by w plus the potential income of the six years $6y_h$, yet she saves on her effort costs $6\,(c_h - c_l)$. The selected δ is lower than in the first-best (5.7), $\delta < \delta^*$, given that outstanding debt exceeds the collected amount during the period of good conduct. As discussed in the ex-post section there is an exception of two marginal cases. First, when debt is fully recovered in all states no distortions will occur. Second, if the remaining working time is insufficient, as discussed in (4.8), the debtor will abstain ex-post and incentives are similar to those of no debt release when $P^{\max} > P$. As noted in the ex-post section these are rather marginal. It is unlikely that a bankruptcy procedure will be successfully initiated at all.

5.3.4 *Proposal*

As under the regulation of no debt release one must distinguish between two cases: whether $P \leq P^{\max}$ or $P > P^{\max}$. The proposal does not change the debtor's effort decision ex-post, i.e. $Y_S = Y_B$. As long as $P \leq P^{\max}$ the incentive structure is similar to 'no debt release,' hence, there are no distortions of the effort choices neither ex-post nor ex-ante. Since the debtor always pays the entire debt, and internalizes all the costs of the credit, as to make the creditor face no risk at all, i.e. $L = D = P$. Distortions in the debtor's ex-ante choice may arise only, when $D > P^{\max}$. The debtor is not willing to pay this amount in case of distress. Hence, because the creditor is not paid the entire sum in all states, he charges a risk premium. Still, this premium will be lower than the one charged under no debt release, since there is no ex-post welfare loss involved. The expected return to the creditor is higher, while the expected net loss in future income incurred on the debtor remains the same.

$$w - \frac{L - P^{\max}}{\delta} = k'(\delta) \tag{5.14}$$

The greater the difference between L and $P^{\max}$, the smaller is the δ that the debtor will choose. Note, that the creditor still receives a considerable (based on the debtor's capabilities) amount in the insolvent state, and the debtor is bound to her reservation utility in case of distress, so that she has little expected gain. This means that for debts exceeding $P^{\max}$ the debtor may choose $\delta < \delta^*$, but it is the least distorting of all discussed regulations.

To summarize: Analyzing the various regulations it is seen that any form of debt release involves some ex-ante deviation from δ^*. Even with no debt release, distortions appear, when debt exceeds a particular amount. Several factors determine the debtor's effort choice ex-ante: Most importantly, it is determined through the magnitude of the credit, the set of payments in the various states and the difference between them. The remaining income at $t = 1$ and the potential loss of future income, and finally the risk premium charged by the creditor. Moreover, it depends on the debtor's personal characteristics, such as her costs of effort or her future income. Again, all of the discussed regulations may induce the debtor to deviate from δ^* given particular circumstances. Yet, the proposed regulation causes the least distortions.

5.4 Extensions

The previous section has shown that any kind of debt release causes the debtor to deviate from δ^*, lowering her precaution against bankruptcy at the expense of the creditor. Yet, the framework employed here is rather narrow. An insolvency is usually a more complex upshot that impairs the essence of the debtor's personal and financial position such as her income prospects, personal belongings or even her standing in society. It is often argued that these personal effects of bankruptcy on the individual even under a debtor friendly regime such as the U.S. Chapter 7 outweighs any potential profit the debtor may expect by far. Therefore, this section discusses possible extensions such as the existence of a collateral, a change in income expectations caused by bankruptcy and the costs of procedure and possible moral connotations of bankruptcy. These extensions of the framework are discussed with respect to their ability to shape both the debtor's decision ex-ante and mitigate the distortion produced by the prospect of debt release. From an intuitive perspective, these would increase the debtor's precaution. This is mostly true, yet, as the analysis reveals, results turn out to be more ambiguous. For instance, the existence of a collateral increases the creditor's collection rate as well as the debtor's precaution. Yet, when considering the personal valuation of the collateral, a welfare loss may result when the debtor is simply deprived of her possession. Also, the existence of social stigma is usually viewed as a positive influence on the debtor's decision, but may even increase distortions in certain cases. That is, that the 'honest' debtor may be deterred from taking credit.

5.4.1 *Collateral*

Up this point the debtor was assumed to be penniless, having no other resource apart from her labor income. Also, the value of the asset bought with the credit had fallen to zero at $t = 0$. This resulted in a zero return for the creditor under Chapter 7. Yet, the provisions regulation allows the creditor to seize the debtor's current non-exempt assets. Even though exemption rates vary considerably across states in the U.S., some return is usually created by the reallocation of the debtor's non-exempt assets.

Although several bankruptcy regulations require the seizure of assets, the subsequent analysis is focused on Ch. 7. Here the seizure of assets is the only, therefore most important, means of regulation. The analysis for the other regulations is analogous. Differences are briefly discussed at the end of this section. These are important to consideration on the effects of renegotiation, chapter choice or any trade-off between assets and future income.

The debtor is now assumed to have bought a durable asset with the loan taken in $t = 0$, which has the value A at $t = 2$. As I am focusing on Ch. 7, $P = A$. Hence, her maximization problem is now $\max_{\delta} \Lambda + A + \delta(w - D + Y_S) + (1-\delta)(Y_S - A) - k(\delta)$ and the creditor's participation constraint changes to $L = \delta D + (1-\delta) A$. Accordingly her first order condition becomes:

$$w - \frac{L - A}{\delta} = k'(\delta). \tag{5.15}$$

This has two effects, first the creditor's collection rate increases in the bad state. Second, the precaution taken by the debtor rises as she is afraid to be deprived of her possessions. Both cause the debtor to increase ex-ante precaution while the creditor lowers the risk premium.

Yet, assets in the debtor's personal possession usually carry personal value. This means, that it is more precious to her than the market value. As a result, if the debtor is deprived of this asset so that it is sold for the market value, welfare loss occurs. To illustrate, the asset has two values; its value to the debtor A^D and its market value A^M, with $D > A^D \geq A^M$. Thus, her incentive compatibility constraint is
$\Lambda + A^D + \delta(w - D + Y_S) + (1-\delta)\left(Y_S - A^D\right)$ and the debtor's first order condition becomes

$$w - D + A^D = k'(\delta). \tag{5.16}$$

When substituting the creditor's participation constraint the welfare loss becomes apparent.

$$w - \frac{L - A^M}{\delta} + \left(A^D - A^M\right) = k'(\delta) \tag{5.17}$$

The term in brackets marks the welfare loss, originating from the fact that the return to the creditor and the loss to the debtor differ. The impact on the risk premium is only A^M while the loss imposed on the debtor is A^D. Hence, when the asset is simply seized, a welfare loss of $A^D - A^M$ occurs to society.

5.4.1.1 *Reaffirmations under Chapter 7*

Introducing the possibility of renegotiations (sometimes referred to as reaffirmations) can improve the situation.[7] In an out-of-court renegotiation the parties may agree to allow the debtor to keep the asset, if she promises to return some negotiated amount out of her future income to the creditor.[8] Depending on each participants' bargaining power this surplus $A^D - A^M$ is distributed among parties.[9] Let $\beta \in [0,1]$ index the debtor's bargaining power, where $\beta = 1$ means that she retains the entire surplus from renegotiations (and pays A^M) and $\beta = 0$ represents the case where the creditor has all the bargaining power and receives the entire ex-post surplus from renegotiations (i.e. the debtor pays A^D).

Renegotiations have several effects aside from the ex-post surplus being realized. Renegotiations increase the creditor's ex-post surplus to

$$P = A^M + (1-\beta)\left(A^D - A^M\right), \tag{5.18}$$

in anticipation - and since he is acting on a competitive market - the risk premium decreases. Yet, a surplus of $\beta\left(A^D - A^M\right)$ rests with the debtor, causing a third effect. The share of the reaffirmation's surplus received by the debtor reduces the harshness of bankruptcy. This reaffirmation may cause her to lower δ. To see the overall effect consider the social surplus (SS), which is the sum of the participants' payoffs

$$SS = \Lambda + \delta\left(w + Y_S + A^D\right) + (1-\delta)\left(A^M + \alpha\left(A^D - A^M\right)\right) - k(\delta) \tag{5.19}$$

where $\alpha \in [0,1]$ represents an index for the effectiveness of renegotiation.

[7] This part of the analysis rests upon Adler, Polak and Schwartz (2000).

[8] For a discussion of reaffirmations see Culhane et. al (1999) and Czarnetzky (2000).

[9] Reaffirmations are often viewed with scepticism and are heavily regulated in the U.S. as debtors are often said to give into unthrifty agreements (see report of the National Bankruptcy Review Comission from October, 20 1997.) http://govinfo.library.unt.edu/nbrc/reporttitlepg.html

When $\alpha = 1$ renegotiations are always successful and when $\alpha = 0$ the opposite is true.

$$MSS = \frac{d(SS)}{d\delta} = w + (1-\alpha)\left(A^D - A^M\right) - k(\delta) \tag{5.20}$$

This states that social surplus rises with higher probabilities of success in renegotiations. In order to understand how the possibility of renegotiations affect social welfare, the social welfare function should be differentiated with respect to α, while absorbing δ as implicitly depending on α, i.e. $\delta(\alpha)$.

$$\frac{d(SS)}{d\alpha} = (1-\delta)\left(A^D - A^M\right) + \frac{d\delta}{d\alpha}\frac{d(SS)}{d\delta}. \tag{5.21}$$

The first term is positive as the two components are positive. I also know that $\frac{d(SS)}{d\delta}$ is positive because the social surplus is rising in the success probability, δ. When $\delta \leq (1-\beta)$ holds $\frac{d\delta}{d\alpha}$ is also positive and hence the overall effect of renegotiations is positive. If $\delta \leq (1-\beta)$ does not hold the effect of renegotiations depends on the relation of the two terms, i.e. whether the surplus generated by the renegotiations $(A^D - A^M)$ is sufficiently large. This can can be summarized as:

Proposition 5.2 *Renegotiation is ex-ante efficient when the default probability is lower than the bargaining power of the creditor, i.e.* $\delta \leq (1-\beta)$.

Proof. To see this consider the debtor's maximization problem

$$\max_{\delta} \Lambda + \delta\left(w - D + A^D\right) + (1-\delta)\alpha\beta\left(A^D - A^M\right) - k(\delta) \tag{5.22}$$

Giving a first order condition of

$$w - D + A^D - \alpha\beta\left(A^D - A^M\right) - k'(\delta) = 0 \tag{5.23}$$

which may be rewritten as

$$w + (1-\alpha)\left(A^D - A^M\right) - k'(\delta) = D - A^M - \alpha(1-\beta)\left(A^D - A^M\right). \tag{5.24}$$

The right hand side of (5.24) represents the marginal social surplus. While the creditor's participation constraint is

$$L = \delta D + (1-\delta)\left(A^M + \alpha(1-\beta)\left(A^D - A^M\right)\right), \tag{5.25}$$

this may be rearranged to

$$D-\left[A^{M}+\alpha(1-\beta)\left(A^{D}-A^{M}\right)\right]=\frac{L-\left[A^{M}+\alpha(1-\beta)\left(A^{D}-A^{M}\right)\right]}{\delta} \tag{5.26}$$

It may be seen that the left hand side of (5.26) and the right hand side of (5.24) coincide. Hence, combining the two equations gives an implicit definition of $\delta(\alpha)$, stating the influence of renegotiations on the failure probability.

$$w+(1-\alpha)\left(A^{D}-A^{M}\right)-k'(\delta)=\frac{L-\left[A^{M}+\alpha(1-\beta)\left(A^{D}-A^{M}\right)\right]}{\delta} \tag{5.27}$$

For this solution to be a maximum the second order condition must be smaller than zero. Thus

$$-k''(\delta)<-\frac{L-\left[A^{M}+\alpha(1-\beta)\left(A^{D}-A^{M}\right)\right]}{\delta^{2}} \tag{5.28}$$

which implies

$$\delta k''(\delta)>\frac{L-\left[A^{M}+\alpha(1-\beta)\left(A^{D}-A^{M}\right)\right]}{\delta} \tag{5.29}$$

The right hand side represents the marginal social surplus (MSS) as stated in (5.27). It remains to be shown when $\frac{d\delta}{d\alpha}$ is positive. This can be found by totally differentiating (5.27) with respect to α. Doing this and rearranging the equation yields:

$$\frac{d\delta}{d\alpha}\left[MSS-\delta k''(\delta)\right]=-\left(A^{D}-A^{M}\right)\left[(1-\beta)-\delta\right]. \tag{5.30}$$

I know from (5.29) that the term in brackets on the left hand side is negative. Since $\left(A^{D}-A^{M}\right)$ is positive (hence negative due to the sign), in order $\frac{d\delta}{d\alpha}$ to be positive the last term in brackets on the right hand side must be positive. This is true so long as $(1-\beta)>\delta$. This means that renegotiation increases social surplus and is, therefore, ex-ante efficient. This proves the proposition. □

Giving some intuition of the results: (5.21) states the overall effect of the renegotiation. The first term states the surplus $(A^{D}-A^{M})$ generated by renegotiations (first effect), whereas the second shows how this surplus is distributed among participants. The second effect is the creditor's expected share, which will cause him to lower the interest rate, and the third effect is the surplus received by the debtor, which eases the harshness of insolvency, and might cause her to lower ex-ante precautions.

When δ is small, i.e. default is a realistic prospect, the second effect will be decisive. The creditor's expected share, $(1-\beta)$, of the ex-post surplus needs to be relatively large for any renegotiation to lower the interest rate and thereby increase the debtor's incentive to remain solvent. The creditor keeps a large share of the surplus and the debtor has a strong incentive to remain solvent. The proposition also states that renegotiation is ex-ante efficient when δ and β are small. Yet, it only states a relation between the success probability and ex-post bargaining power. This means that a renegotiation which does not satisfy the inequality may still be efficient, if the surplus created is large enough. In other words, the renegotiation need not satisfy the proposition if the first effect is large enough. Regarding (5.21) all renegotiations which satisfy the inequality have a positive effect; for those that don't it depends whether the first term or the second is larger.

5.4.1.2 *Reaffirmations and Out-of-Court Negotiations under other Regulations*

With regulations other than U.S. Chapter 7, the scope for renegotiations is limited. These regulations already compel the debtor to assign a considerable part of her future income to the creditor. As a result, the debtor has less future income to offer in return for keeping her assets. Especially when $P = P^{max}$, the debtor has almost nothing to offer.[10]

Yet, achieving an out-of-court agreement could, for example, save procedural costs. An agreement could be achieved before the actual procedure is started. The procedural costs are usually considerable for both parties.[11]

[10] Remember that P^{max} does not leave the debtor with a zero income, she is still compensated for her private costs, and therefore receives a positive income. So if an asset is sufficiently precious to the debtor she might still engage in renegotiations, and offer the creditor part of her remaining income. Yet, the creditor may be reluctant to agree as later income becomes increasingly uncertain.

[11] The procedural costs are usually considerable. For instance, when the German insolvency regulation was introduced in 1999, many debtors were excluded from debt release because they could not afford the costs of procedure. After an extensive discussion among legal scholars and professionals the law was changed allowing those debtors to apply for legal aid. Yet, this was in fact only a deferral of payment, as this aid had to be repaid. This claim by the state is assigned the highest priority and even persists four years beyond the period of good conduct. Only if the debtor could not manage during those nine years to pay, this debt is also released. (see InsO § 4a-d) For a consideration of the effects of

A potential surplus may be realized, as the costs of procedure neither increase the debtor's nor the creditor's return. The creditor may save on his direct costs, such as collection expenses or the costs of a court procedure. The debtor saves on her part of the procedural costs. When outstanding debt is sufficiently high, the regulation gathers the debtor's entire ex-post surplus. Here, the costs of procedure are directly decreasing the creditor's return. The analysis is analogous to the one conducted for reaffirmations under Chapter 7 and will therefore not be carried out in detail. As under Ch. 7, depending on the distribution of bargaining power, β, and the default probability, the debtor might be tempted to lower δ ex-ante in contrast to other regulations. Yet, given the harshness of the regulation and the amount she is already pledged to pay, distortions should only occur in marginal configurations.

5.4.2 *Changes in Income Expectations*

So far it is assumed that the shock only destroys current wealth, w, and has no effect on the debtor's future income expectations, i.e. $Y_S = Y_B$. The only exception was a decline resulting from adjustments to the debtor's effort level as a response to the bankruptcy regulation. One may challenge this assumption. Distress is a major draw back in the life of the debtor, effecting not only the debtor's immediate wealth but also future income expectations. For instance, insolvency may be caused by unemployment, a change in the debtor's family situation or illness. Hence, it is now assumed that $Y_B < Y_S$. Any such event is likely to also corrupt the debtor's future income expectations.

As such circumstances harm primarily the debtor herself, she would wish to raise precautions: assuming that she has influence on the incidence. This would mitigate the distortions caused by the prospect of debt release.

$$w - D + P + Y_S - Y_B = k'(\delta) \tag{5.31}$$

The first effect in this equation is that a reduction in distress rises as $Y_S - Y_B > 0$, and hence $k'(\delta)$ and δ rises. Yet, the shock could have occurred without the loan, i.e. the debtor's first order condition without credit must be preemptively adapted,

$$w + Y_S - Y_B = k'(\delta). \tag{5.32}$$

out-of-court renegotiation see Huls (1997) and Krüger (2000).

Even without the credit which defines the first best, the debtor would have already raised precautions, i.e. the δ^* as a point of reference is different.

Yet, credit itself has a negative effect. This is present in (5.31). As P is depending on debtor's post-bankruptcy income, Y_B, the creditor's collection rate is lower. As a result he will have to raise D, see (5.4), depending on the magnitude of income change, $Y_S - Y_B$. This diminishes the debtor incentive to stay solvent. To emphasize, when her post bankruptcy return falls to zero, $Y_B - P = 0$, the incentives to stay solvent are declining rapidly.

Though a decline in post bankruptcy income causes the debtor to raise precautions in general, taking credit does not improve her incentives to remain solvent.

5.4.3 *Stigma and other Non-Monetray Penalties*

As discussed in chapter 2 and section 4.4.3 non-monetrary penalties are often implemented. Several bankruptcy codes impose various restrictions on the debtor as part of the requirement for debt release -instead of monetary requirements. These restrictions aim at a re-education or supervision of the debtor, rather than at increasing the creditors satisfaction rate. Such instruments are already explored in the ex-post analysis (see section 4.4.3) and are found to be of limited benefit ex-post. Yet, they should be beneficial ex-ante as these increase the disutility from default and consequentially increase the debtor's precaution ex-ante.

An individual's decision is not only determined by monetary values, it is influenced by other means such as social stigma or other forms of social wigging. A moral obligation to pay ones debt is be found in many cultures. In many countries or U.S. states, a social stigma is associated with bankruptcy proceedings. Bankrupt people are considered to have done something insidious.

Many regulations rely on the consumer's concern for upholding a reputation for paying debt, i.e. credit history. Such credit files, especially the bankruptcy flag appearing up to ten years post a bankruptcy, have assessable monetary consequences as they may damage future credit.[12] As

[12] For an analysis on the influence of the bankruptcy flag on consumers' eligibility for credits see Musto (1999). Musto finds that the existence of a bankruptcy flag does not bar the consumer completly from any further credit, it is instead sometimes interpreted as slight positive sign, as a debtor fresh out of bankruptcy is presumed to have only few other obligations.

shown by Fisher et al. (2004) consumers exhibit excess sensitivity to such a bankruptcy flag.

Influence of stigma, increases the disutility in the bankrupt state, which increases the incentives for the debtor to remain solvent. Various views exist on the disutility resulting from the social stigma of bankruptcy. For example, it may be seen as a fixed amount which is -in a way- experienced per distress. Alternatively it may be dependent on the magnitude of the penalty, i.e. the more years the debtor expects to spend in the period of good conduct, the higher the expected disutility. Assume that d is the disutility that the debtor experiences in case of bankruptcy. This d is dependent on the magnitude of the penalty $d(P)$, with $d'(P) > 0$. Hence her first order condition changes accordingly

$$w - D + P + d(P) = k'(\delta) \tag{5.33}$$

The presence of disutility accelerates the debtor's precaution against bankruptcy. This seems to be a desirable result for it provides an easy way out of the dilemma between ex-ante and ex-post efficiency. Just promote the stigma of bankruptcy and ex-ante distortions will vanish. This is true, under the assumption that stigma does not produce any undesirable side-effects such as distorting the debtor's economic incentives ex-post. Though the amount of disutility may vary with the harshness of the penalty, the disutility perceived is a matter of the debtor's personal social background.

Beyond a social obligation to fulfill one's financial obligation, there are also moral connotations. For instance, most religions either implicitly or even explicitly demand their faithful to comply to contracts; debt contracts in particular. Jewish tradition places a very strong moral obligation on repaying one's debt. According to Islamic religion God is a witness to any contract entered into by individuals.[13] Similar provisions are be found in Hinduism where defaulting debtors are threatened to be reincarnated in a lower cast. The Buddhist faith commands the payment of debt before the commencement of the new year.[14] Christians are also generally demanded to meet their obligations, while still forgiving debtors who lie victim to inauspicious circumstances.[15] Drawing from this, it follows that

[13] Yet, Judaism also knows debt forgiving in the Jubilee. (see Deut, 15, 1-11)

[14] See Efrat (1998) for a discussion of the implications of moral and religious connotations of bankruptcy.

[15] see Mat, 18, 21-35.

the debtor's socialization and belief system greatly determine the disutility brought about by debt. Stigma or moral obligation is not directly by the patterns of law. Unfortunately, stigma cannot be engineered so as to guarantee sufficient precaution. If there is too much stigma, the debtor will be deterred from taking the credit. In other words, the function with which the penalty, P, is processed is an individual matter. This perception is beyond the influence of the law-maker and may even have adverse consequences.

In the literature on consumer bankruptcy it is often argued that there are two types of defaulting debtors, those whose bankruptcy was thrusted upon them, and those who take advantage of the bankruptcy provisions and default maliciously. Assume the two types cannot be distinguished by the creditors. It is suspected that the first type is more responsive to non-monetary penalties such as stigma. Those who go bankrupt opportunistically are less likely to follow other social norms. Furthermore, opportunistic debtors are less sensitive to the stigma associated with bankruptcy and will, consequently, choose lower precaution. In an extreme only the shirkers will take credit, making credit more costly, and finally push obedient debtors out of the credit market. This 'market for lemons' results from the from the difficulty of adjusting stigma in order to achieve a desired outcome. Hence, promoting stigma deters individuals who are sensitive to stigma from taking credit, while leaving 'shirkers' immune to such a threat. When the obedient debtors drop out of the market, creditors are left with a lowered earning potential. Although, this 'market for lemons'[16] argument may be exaggerated, it provides logic against the assumption that stigma always has positive effects on bankruptcy regulation.

To sum up: Social stigma is capable of mitigating the distorting effect of debt release for the moral obligation to pay one's debt is present in most societies. Suffering from stigma may pose a greater threat to people than the consequences of the actual regulation. Yet, stigma should be handled with care for several reasons. First it is endogenous within the society and is therefore hard to influence, so there can be no certainty whether the proper amount of stigma is imposed on the individual. Because stigma is discerned different across individuals, only those who are immune to the result may take credit.

[16] see Ackerlof (1970)

5.5 Numerical Example

The analysis in the pervious section shows that any kind of debt release is capable of distorting the debtor's effort ex-ante. This section evaluates the magnitude of these effects by using representative numbers, building on the Numeric Example presented in the ex-post chapter. This method is the sensible tool to compare the effects of the various regulations, given the lack of statistical data and the profound differences between the environments of the discussed regulations. The study focuses on how the level of debt-repayment (D) varies with an increase in the size of the loan (L). This represents the contract the debtor will be offered for a particular seize of credit. This is because the creditor's only latitude in the credit contract is D. The creditor raises D in response to a higher risk of distress and a decreased satisfaction rate, P. Put differently, D represents the the risk premium charged by the creditor. The higher the disparity between L and D, the greater is the distorting effect of that regulation ex-ante. The debtor's participating decision (whether to take the loan) is driven by the benefit Λ. This implies that when the risk premium becomes rather large, the debtor will be unlikely to take the credit, it is equally possible also that the creditors will refrain from extending loan to the debtor.

Based on the evaluations in the ex-post chapter, the following numbers are assumed: The post-bankruptcy income is set to $Y_S = 52,800€$ and pre-bankruptcy wealth is $w = 70,000€$. The reason for assuming $w > Y_S$ is to arrive at situations where debt release is ex-post necessary. The relation $L \leq w$ is set, so the debtor is capable of paying her entire debt off in the solvent state, as debt is due in full at $t = 0$. Furthermore, I assume for post-bankruptcy income $y_h - c_h = 4,400€$ and $y_l - c_l = 2,800€$. Remaining working time after $t = 0$ is twelve periods, which means $Y_S = 12 * y_h = 52,800$. From this the payments in the bankrupt state can be deduced:

	Y_B	max. P w/o dist.	P
Ch.7	52,800	0	0
no debt release	$52,800 \vee 0$	52,800	$L \vee 0$
Ger. Reg.	$52,800 \vee 43,200$	34,800	$L \vee 34,800$
Proposal	52,800	52,800	$L \vee 52,800$
mod. Prop.	52,800	40,000	$L \vee 40,000$

On the table above, the four discussed regulations are listed, and the last row comprises a modified form of the proposal. Here the maximal

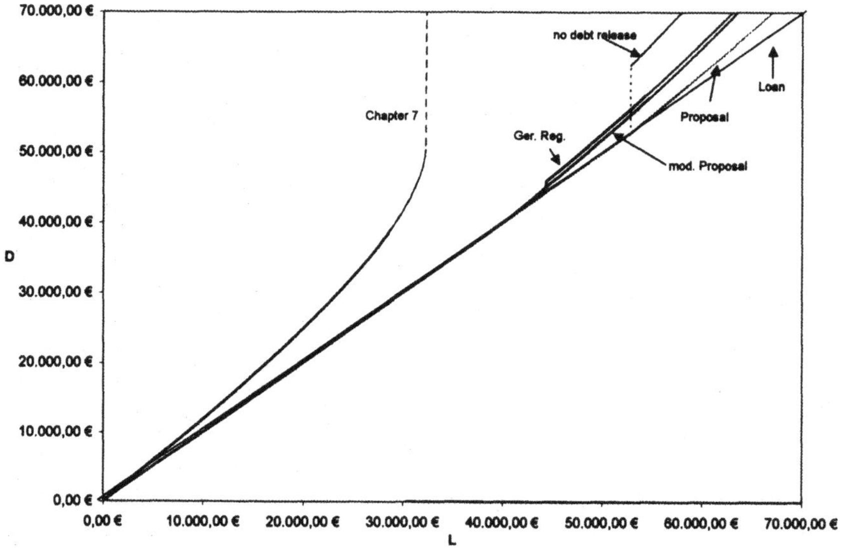

Fig. 5.2 The graph represents the distortions created by the various bankruptcy regulations ex-ante

amount is limited to 40,000€, which adds up to an expected duration of 4,25 years of payment. I introduce this modified proposed to account for the possible distortions discussed in section 4.3.1. In this case the debtor retains an expected surplus of 12,000€. The first column displays the post bankruptcy income resulting from the three existing regulations and two forms of the proposed regulation. When a regulation comprises distortions ex-post, two possible post-bankrutpcy incomes arise. The second row indicates the maximum amount for which the regulation remains undistorted, i.e. where $D = P$, and consequently the first income in row one applies. The last row gives the creditor's return. This consists of two values for two different events. First when the debtor pays the entire sum even in case of distress, i.e. when L does not exceed the amount displayed in the second column, and second, when the debt bankruptcy regulation is applied thereby demanding some maximum amount from the debtor.

According to the analysis, the debtor's choice of δ is dependent on her first order condition as stated in (5.8). The assumed cost function is $k(\delta) = -x\delta \ln(\delta - 1)$, and the derivative is accordingly $k'(\delta) = \frac{x\delta}{(1-\delta)}$. Where x

is some parameter that determines the curvature of the function. This cost function satisfies the properties set up in the ex-ante setting.[17] It is convenient to set $x = 11,000$. Using these parameters and analyzing an $L \in [0; 70,000]$ the following graph results. With these parameters the first best probability is set to $\delta^* = 0.8642$. The graph below states the relationship between D development and a rising L under each of the various bankruptcy regulations. The bisecting line, represents the seize of the loan L.

The graph illustrates that as the loan rises, the required debt payment rises in equal proportion so long as debt is paid in full in both states. When the payments start to differ, the creditor has to demand an increased D-in order to insure his participation. For Chapter 7 it can be seen that D rapidly rises and then accelerates to infinity when the loan exceeds 32, 300€. For that sum a debt payment of 51, 000€ would be demanded (when $P = 0$). Yet, at that stage a credit contract would not be offered any more, as those conditions violate the assumption that the debtor's expected income is sufficient to cover the payment. In this case the $D-$curve changes into a dotted lime. No debt release is another interesting case. Here the there are no distortions up to $P \leq P^{\max} = 52,800$€, and then there is a discontinuity in the debt payment, it jumps at 52, 799€ (here $D = P = L$) to 62, 419€ for a loan of 52, 000€. It is interesting to note that no credit would be offered as soon as D deviates from L. Though the German regulation entails a welfare loss ex-post, ex-ante distortions seem to remain quite moderate. Again the welfare loss inherent in the regulation can also be witnessed in the graph as D leaps up from 44, 399€ to 45, 943€ for an additional Euro of credit. Yet, the risk premium remains moderate, as D only rises at a slightly increased rate compared to L. As a result the German regulation outperforms the no debt release regulations for higher values of L. Though, there is no welfare loss inherent in the regulation, the modified proposal features similar characteristics. The amount collected by the creditor is higher, while the expected length is shorter (only 4,25 years). Consequently the increase in risk premium rests below the German regulation. For the proposal there are no distortions until $P^{\max}$ is reached, afterwards D rises

[17] A suitable cost function should have the following properties *(i)* $k(0) = 0$, *(ii)* $\lim_{\delta \to 1} k(\delta) = \infty$, *(iii)*$k'(\delta) > 0$.These conditions *(i)* - *(iii)* insure $k''(\delta) > 0$, and hence concavity of $k(\delta)$ in $[0, 1)$.

at a moderate rate. This demonstrates again, that the proposed regulation creates the least distortions of all considered regulations.

5.6 Risk Attitude

The previous analysis shows that any kind of debt release may prompt the debtor to take less precaution against bankruptcy. In doing so, the debtor attempts to externalize part of the costs of the credit upon the creditor. This would suggest that the proportion of bankruptcy petition is rather large. Yet, this is not what actually occurs. Also, from an intuitive perspective this result is not entirely convincing, considering the advantage an individual debtor expects, when her entire future income is at stake. This result may be rooted in the risk neutrality assumption. In order, to examine whether alternating this assumption would produce any new qualitative results, the debtor's risk attitude is placed under disquisition. This section first examines the behavior of a debtor who is risk averse in the von Neumann and Morgenstern sense. The assumption is then changed in order to investigate how a boundedly rational individual would asses default probabilities, and consequentially, take precautions to avoid distress.

Though, one may think that a risk averse debtor exercises more precaution, and hence, distortions would disappear, this does not result from the analysis. Instead, results suggest that the debtor will exert less precaution because the loan offers her the possibility to lower the variance of income realization. Even if the credit lowers her expected payoff, it will grant her higher expected utility, since the credit allows her to reduce the variance of he income realizations. Introducing the notion of bounded rationality into the analysis a mitigation of the ex-ante distortions may be accomplished. First time dependent choice is considered, based on the idea that the benefit Λ is of secondary importance when the debtor decides on her effort at $t = 1$. Using this prudence the distortions may be overcome. The same effect may be found when using the 'reference point.' The section closes with a brief discussion of the effects of a boundedly rational actor who misjudges the effects of a credit contract on her future income, because she is only capable of limited calculations. Consideration is made on the notion of trapped debtor who signed a credit contract under duress and then faces negative consequences.

5.6.1 *Risk Aversion*

It is often argued that the institutions of debt discharge provide the consumer a partial wealth insurance.[18] In general a risk averse consumer prefers a certain outcome. In the absence of such outcome she would at least attempt to equalize her wealth across states. Hence, she benefits from a reduction of her wealth in the good state in return for an increase in the bad state. The individual consumer is averse to income shocks and therefore desires to ease the risk of distress. Consequentially, she places a high value on regulated debt release, as it offers her an opportunity to counter the inconsistencies of life.

The debtor is now assumed to be risk averse, having an additively separable, strictly concave utility function for income $U(Y)$, with $U' > 0, U'' < 0$. She maximizes utility as follows:

$$\max_{\delta} \delta U (w - D + Y_S + \Lambda) + (1 - \delta) U (Y_B - P + \Lambda) - k(\delta). \tag{5.34}$$

Yielding a first order condition of

$$U (w - D + Y_S + \Lambda) - U (Y_B - P + \Lambda) = k'(\delta) \tag{5.35}$$

or in short:

$$U_{Sc} - U_{Bc} = k'(\delta). \tag{5.36}$$

This states, again, that marginal benefit should equal marginal costs. Where U_{Sc} denotes the utility in the solvent state with credit and U_{Bc} the debtor's utility in the bankrupt state with a credit, U_{Snc} and U_{Bnc} represent the utility in the two states when no credit was taken. The condition (5.36) indicates that now the differences in utility in the two states is critical. This means that not only the monetary difference under risk neutrality matter, but also the placement within the utility function. Under risk neutrality her utility consists of her present and future income minus the debt payment in the good state. Now, the non-monetary utility, Λ, derived from the loan is relevant. She still enjoys the benefit (as it is assumed to be fully consumed

[18] see e.g. Adler, Polak and Schwartz (2000), Jacoby (2002).

in $t = 1$) and has to pay P from her future income during the bankrupt state. Note, that the benefit of the loan Λ persists in the derivative and increases the debtor's utility in both states.

For reference, consider the debtor's maximization problem without credit. Here, her first order condition is:

$$U_{Snc} - U_{Bnc} = k'(\delta) \tag{5.37}$$
$$U(w + Y_s) - U(Y_S) = k'(\delta). \tag{5.38}$$

Solved for δ (5.37) determines the optimal level of precaution, δ^*.

Also remember that the debtor expects to be at least as well off with the credit than without. Otherwise, taking the credit would not have been rational. This is derived from her *participation constraint*:

$$E(U_c) \geq E(U_{nc}) \Rightarrow \tag{5.39}$$

or this can be rewritten in more detail as:

$$\begin{aligned} &\delta U(w - D + Y_S + \Lambda) + (1-\delta) U(Y_B - P + \Lambda) - k(\delta) \\ &\geq \delta^* U(w + Y_S) + (1-\delta^*) U(Y_B) - k(\delta^*) \end{aligned} \tag{5.40}$$

The participation constraint determines the magnitude of the benefit Λ. She expects to be at least as well off with the credit than without it.

To see how the debtor adjusts δ due to the credit, I need to evaluate how the utility of the various states is changed by the credit. As opposed to risk neutrality, the debtor's decision is not only determined by the difference between the good and the bad state, but also on the value of utility she derives from either state, i.e. Λ persists in the derivative. Here four combinations are possible, depending upon whether her utility in the various states rises or falls due to the loan. In other words, either she has higher or lower income as compared to her situation without credit:

(1) $(U_{Bnc} < U_{Bc}) \wedge (U_{Sc} < U_{Snc})$
(2) $(U_{Bnc} < U_{Bc}) \wedge (U_{Sc} > U_{Snc})$
(3) $(U_{Bnc} > U_{Bc}) \wedge (U_{Sc} < U_{Snc})$
(4) $(U_{Bnc} > U_{Bc}) \wedge (U_{Sc} > U_{Snc})$

Following, these cases are evaluated in detail. First, by checking whether they are possible under the given assumptions, then by appraising how likely they are to occur, and finally, evaluating the consequences that these have upon δ. For completeness, it should be noted that it is also possible that the utility in the good and bad state is not altered by credit. Here, her effort decision would not change so that no distortions result. For example, this would happen if debt is paid in full in all states and the benefit of the loan coincides with the payments, i.e. $P = D = L = \Lambda$.

For the analysis it should be noted that the difference in wealth for each state has a proportional ordering of corresponding utility. Because a utility function is a positive monotonous transformation, the order is preserved. The order of the various realizations depends also on the magnitude of Λ, i.e. it determines which of the above cases is applicable.

Upon consideration of these cases it becomes apparent that the third and the fourth case are rather unlikely to occur in this present setup. In the **third case,** the debtor gets a lower utility in the good *and* in the bad state. Thus, I can infer from the first inequality that for the bad state[19] $Y_S - P + \Lambda < Y_S \Rightarrow \Lambda < P$ and from the second inequality I get $w + Y_S - D + \Lambda < w + Y_s \Rightarrow \Lambda < D$. The benefit derived from the credit is rather negligible, $\Lambda < P \leq D$. Checking for assumption (5.5) the above is possible. Yet, it would hardly fulfill the debtor's participation constraint, it would not be in her own interest to take the credit. She would get a lower utility in both, therefore, she would have to raise δ considerably in order to ensure that her expected utility increases. Yet, this would increase costs and thus violate the participation constraint.

The **fourth case** is also not likely to occur. Here by taking the credit the debtor increases the variance of her income realization. In general, she may still derive a higher expected utility. Yet, considering the income realizations shows that $Y_S - P + \Lambda < Y_S \Rightarrow \Lambda < P$ and $w + Y_S - D + \Lambda > w + Y_s \Rightarrow \Lambda > D$. This means $P > \Lambda > D$, which is hardly possible as it would violate assumption (5.5). This is true if the bankruptcy regulation is non-distorting.

When the regulation causes distortions ex-post, as for example 'no debt release,' results do not change. The argument is similar to the one made for no debt release under risk neutrality. When $P > P^{max}$ future income falls to $Y_B = P = 0$. And from the inequalities I get $\Lambda < Y_S$ and $\Lambda > D$, which implies $Y_S > D$. This is not possible in the present setup, since her future income would be insufficient to pay the debts even in the solvent

[19] Assuming the bankruptcy rule is ex-post undistorting.

state, $D = P > Y_{S/B} = P^{\max}$. Hence, the forth case may be excluded.

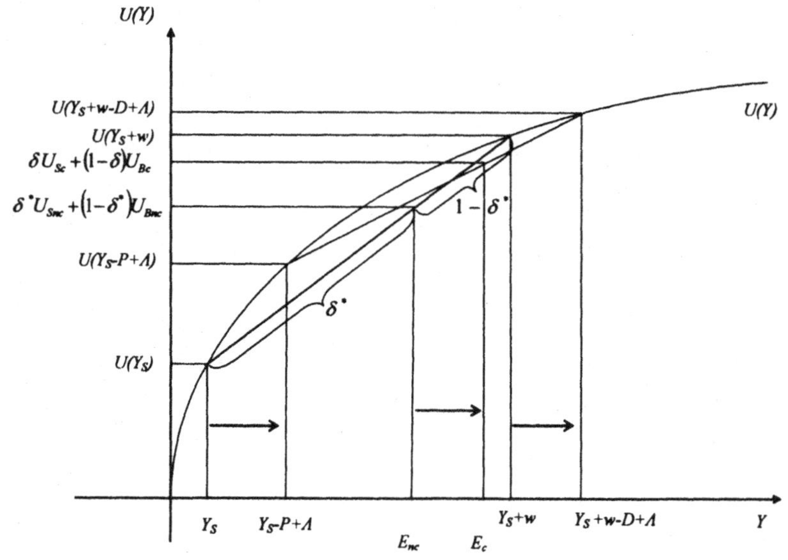

Fig. 5.3 Taking the credit shifts the debtor's income realizations to the right, thereby decreasing the variance, $P \leq D \leq \Lambda$.

Turning to the **second case** for the analysis, this case seems to be more likely. Here the credit raises the debtor's utility in both states, i.e. her decision is shifted to the right on her utility function. From the inequality I get: $Y_S < Y_S - P + \Lambda$ and $w + Y_S < w + Y_S - D + \Lambda$. This implies that $P < \Lambda$ and $D < \Lambda$, which means that the benefit is larger than the payment in either state. This is possible within the present setup. Also, the debtor will participate, because her entire decision problem is shifted to the right. This implies that she will always receive a higher expected utility with the credit than without it for each δ. Therefore, taking credit always benefits he debtor. Last, I examine the consequences for δ. The decision is determined by (5.36), which states that it is determined by the differences in utility in the two states. Due to the patterns of the cost function[20], the higher the

[20] Remember that $k(\delta)$ is strictly increasing in δ and so is $k'(\delta) > 0$, and $k''(\delta) > 0$. This means the higher the δ the higher are the costs, but also the other way around, the higher the costs (as determined by the first order condition) the higher the δ will be.

difference between the states, the higher the δ chosen by the debtor. So to determine how a credit affects the debtor's precautions in the second case, I need to examine how the difference in utilities plays out to the case with no credit. There are several effects, which are also reflected in Figure 5.3. First, the benefit Λ shifts both monetary realizations to the right by the same distance. Due the concavity of the function, the difference in utility of those monetary realizations declines, i.e. $(U_{Snc} - U_{Bnc} > U_{Sc} - U_{Bc})$. This effect lowers δ, The second effect is the debt payment, which shifts each payoff back to the left. Yet, since $P \leq D$ the payoff in the good state is either shifted by exactly the same distance ($P = D$), or further ($P < D$) to the left than the payoff in the bad state. The difference in payoffs as well as the utility derived from these payoffs declines. Hence, when the credit increase the debtor's utility in both states, she will always respond by decreasing her effort, $\delta < \delta^*$.

Finally, in the **first case** the utility in the bad state increases while the utility in the good case declines. As a result, the variance between the two states declines. Contingent on the parameters the expected income with credit can either be above or below the one without, i.e. $E_{nc} \gtreqless E_c$. When $E_{nc} < E_c$ the argument is analog to the second case, and the debtor's efforts against distress will decline. In the other case $E_{nc} > E_c$ it may still be rational for the debtor to take credit, as it will increase her expected utility. This is represented in Figure 5.4. This case is possible within in the present parameters as the inequalities imply $P < \Lambda < D$, given that the bankruptcy regulation is non-distorting. Whether the participation constraint (5.40) is met depends on the parameters, i.e. not all possible values of D and P will be beneficial for the debtor to take on credit. Given that her participation constraint is met, she will decrease her precaution against distress. This is because the credit shifts both realizations inwards which reduces the variance of income realizations. Since the difference across the realizations determines δ, a smaller differences imply smaller δ. It is convenient to summarize these results in a proposition.

Proposition 5.3 *When the debtor is risk averse and $P \leq L \leq D$, a credit contract will always incite her to lower her ex-ante precaution, i.e.* $\delta < \delta^*$.

Proof. As it was shown above only the first and the second case are possible in the present setup. The debtor chooses δ depending on her first order condition (5.36), this indicates that her effort decision at $t = 1$

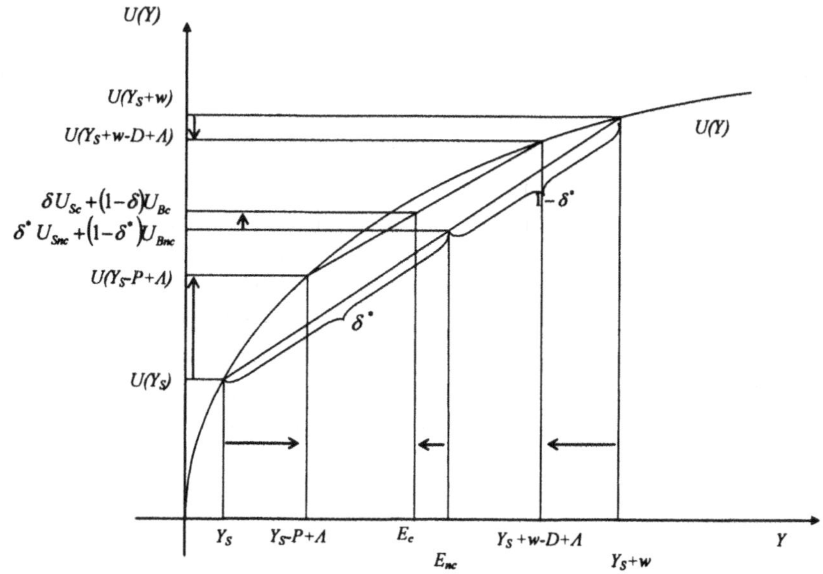

Fig. 5.4 Taking the credit enables the debtor to choose the variance in income realizations, and is thus beneficial to her, even if the credit provides no extra benefit to her.

depends exclusively on the difference in utility between the two states. Due to the patterns of the cost function $k(\delta)$, which is strictly increasing in δ, with $k' > 0$ and $k'' > 0$, the higher the difference in utility is the greater the δ that the debtor chooses. Or equivalently, the higher is the precaution against distress she will take. Hence, as long as

$$U_{Sc} - U_{Bc} > U_{Snc} - U_{Bnc} \tag{5.41}$$

holds, she will take less precaution with credit than without. Condition (5.41) always holds for the first case. Two effects are present in the second case. First the realizations are shifted to the right by Λ, this decreases the disparity between utilities due to concavity of the utility function, and second the differences in income declines since $P \leq D$, which also lowers the difference between utilities. □

The figure 9 also displays another interesting effect. Here though the expected value declines due to the credit ($E_{nc} > E_c$), the expected utility rises ($U(E_c) > U(E_{nc})$). Had the debtor been risk neutral she would not have signed the contract. Yet, since she is risk averse, reducing the benefit of income realizations increases her utility. This is an effect usually observed when discussing the benefits of an insurance.[21] Only here the setup is slightly different. First the credit is meant to allow the consumer to shift consumption between periods. The insurance function of the bankruptcy code as appraised by various scholars aims at not putting the debtor into debt bondage once she is in distress, but to offer a way out. It is not meant to increase the debtor's wealth in the bad state compared to the no credit situation. Instead of paying the risk premium up front it is included in D, and so only paid in the good state. It is rather straight forward that this effect would further increase distortions.

To sum up: Though a risk averse individual is usually more sensitive to poor income realization, the analysis has shown that the introduction of risk aversion did not abate distortions. Since the benefit derived from the credit is now relevant to the debtor's decision on δ, her payoffs are increased by the credit and she requires less δ due to the concavity of the utility function. With certain thriftless regulations, the debtor is even able to profit from the reduced variance in income realizations. Then her situation is better than that with no credit.

5.6.2 *Time Dependent Choice*

One may argue that since the benefit of the credit is assumed to be rather short lived, it is not relevant for the decision. The debtor fully consumes the benefit at $t = 1$, in the present setup. For example, imagine that the loan pays for a trip to Hawaii and only upon her return she begins working to pay the debt. In this case the actual decision on δ is taken in $t = 1$ *after* the consumer has chosen to take the credit *and* has already consumed the benefit of the credit, Λ. Hence, her choice changes, she is left only with the costs, when deciding on how much effort to put into generating income. She realizes that in the solvent state she now will have $U(w - D + Y_S)$, while in the bad state she may be worse off (having only $U(Y_B - P)$), compared $U(Y_S)$ to the situation without credit. The ex-post analysis has shown that distress sometimes causes serious distortions to future income expectations.

[21] For a discussion on risk aversion and insurance see for example Mas-Colell, Whinston, Green (1995) p. 187.

Her choice at $t = 1$ is now constituted by the first order condition:

$$U(w - D + Y_S) - U(Y_B - P) = k'(\delta) \tag{5.42}$$

Compared to (5.37) her wealth position and her utility is shifted to the left in each state. Therefore, this setup represents the **third case** $[(U_{Bc} < U_{Bnc}) \wedge (U_{Sc} < U_{Snc})]$ as outlined in the previous section. There are several effects present which contribute to this result. First contingent on the magnitude of debt release, i.e. the difference between D and P, which reduces the variance of income realizations. The second effect is a shift of both realizations to the left. As the concavity of the utility function increases, the difference between the states and hence the chosen δ is higher. The relative magnitude of the two effects depends on several factors. The chosen effort will be smaller, the more generous the debt release is and the smaller the future income expectations, Y_S, are. Her decision on δ also depends on the slope of the utility function. If the inequality (5.41) fails to hold she will always raise δ. She is likely to increase her effort unless the debt release regulation is very generous.

Note, that the debtor could have taken the increased effort at $t = 1$ into account when deciding on the credit (i.e. there must not necessarily have been a calculating error or some bounded rationality behavior, though, this is also possible). She estimates the benefit of the credit as large and then chooses to take the credit. This constitutes her participation constraint in $t = 0$, which means that Λ must have have been sufficiently large to guarantee participation.

Another interesting effect arises when the asset is assumed to be durable consumer good such as a car or a house. Then the debtor will lose a potential benefit that she would have enjoyed in later periods. Accordingly, the benefit $\Lambda = \Lambda_{t<2} + \Lambda_{t\geq 2}$ is now split into two parts with $\Lambda_{t<2}$ being the benefit consumed by the debtor before $t = 2$ and $\Lambda_{t\geq 2}$ represents the benefit the debtor expects to derive from the asset in later periods $t \geq 2$. Under this assumption the **fourth case,** as defined in the previous section, becomes possible, i.e. $(U_{Bc} < U_{Bnc}) \wedge (U_{Snc} < U_{Sc})$. Assuming a non-distorting regulation ($Y_S = Y_B$) the condition gives $\Lambda > D$ and $\Lambda_{t<2} < P$. This is possible if the benefit at later periods $\Lambda_{t\geq 2}$ is sufficiently large. Her first order condition now becomes:

$$U(w - D + Y_S + \Lambda) - U(Y_S - P + \Lambda_{t<2}) = k'(\delta). \qquad (5.43)$$

The variance between income realization is now increasing and will always be larger than without a credit, i.e. $U_{Sc} - U_{Bc} > U_{Snc} - U_{Bnc}$. Accordingly, the debtor will always raises δ, $\delta > \delta^*$. So if the consumer good provides sufficient benefits in later periods as well, the debtor will increase her effort to avoid distress.

5.6.3 *Bounded Rationality*

So far, except for the discussion of the effects of stigma, the debtor's decision is based only on monetary parameters and is considered to be perfectly rational. Yet, it may occur to someone investigating consumer choice that the assumption of pure rationality does not always hold. The means by which consumer credit is advertised raises doubt on the presumption that credit is supplied to meet rational interests. Therefore, for exploring consumer choice it may be advantageous to use bounded rationality. Yet, bounded rationality does not offer a coherent theory, at least not yet.[22] It is a broad path of reason with many and partly contradicting theories. Reviewing and applying these theories is beyond the scope of this paper. Therefore, this analysis confines itself to a reevaluation of section 5.6.1, using the notion prospect theory. Here, I focus on the so called 'isolation effect' deducted from previous observations in several experiments by Kahneman and Tversky (1979).[23] They claim that an individual subject tends to conduct decisions by discarding all elements common to the alternatives. When the debtor is choosing her effort at $t = 1$, she only considers the uncertain component of the alternatives that are affected by her income choice. As a result, the benefit from the loan Λ is not affected by her choices, and hence, would not be included in her calculations. According to the predictions of the Prospect Theory, the individual discards all components that are common to the offered prospects in the so called 'editing

[22] See for example Rubinstein "It is difficult to pinpoint any economic work not based on fully rational microeconomic behavior that yields results as rich, deep and interesting as those achieved by standard models assuming full rationality." Runbinstein (1998) p.3. For an overview of the theories of bounded rationality see for instance Rubinstein (1998) and Selten (1999).

[23] A similar effect was found by Fishburn (1977) and named 'reference point'.

phase,' and then rests only with the uncertain parts. In terms of the model, this means that the benefit from the credit, Λ, and (in case the regulation is non-distorting) her future income, Y_S, are discarded. As a reference point the debtor chooses her current wealth position in $t = 1$, i.e. after receiving the benefit and before choosing δ. Kahneman and Tversky also observed a slightly different attitude towards risk. They believe that individuals are risk averse to gains and risk loving with respect to losses. Based on this assumption, using the simplest form of a utility function, the debtor ha the following maximization problem:

$$\max_{\delta} \delta U(w - D) + (1 - \delta) U(-P) - k(\delta) \tag{5.44}$$

The maximization problem differs from (5.36) in so far that the components shared among the different realizations were eliminated from the decision function. Assuming the simplest form of a utility function, i.e. risk neutral for gains and risk averse at some parameter μ for losses, with $\mu > 1$. I arrive at

$$\max_{\delta} \delta(w - D) + (1 - \delta) \mu(-P) - k(\delta) . \tag{5.45}$$

Forming the first order condition, where she bases her decision on yields:

$$w - D + \mu P = k'(\delta) . \tag{5.46}$$

The weight of the penalty in the debtor's decision function increased. Kahneman and Tversky suggest that the parameter μ should be set in a range of $\mu \in [2; 2.5]$. This suggests that the penalty designed by the bankruptcy regulation is perceived by the individual to be equal to at least two times its actual monetary value. As a result, the individual debtor would now choose a much higher δ, even with a considerable debt release. For example with an $\alpha = 2$, the optimal δ^* is chosen if $P = \frac{1}{2}D$, suggesting that losses hurt the debtor much more than gains benefit her. As a result, the debtor will even work harder, compared to her situation without the credit. This result reflects the notion that the threat of being deprived of your personal possession may accelerates your endeavors to prevent this from happening.

The debtor must not necessarily pay back everything or to give up her entire future surplus, in order to maintain ex-ante efficiency. Instead the threat of loosing a considerable portion of future income provides sufficient menace.

Yet, in order to arrive at such a situation the debtor must have decided to take the credit beforehand. One may argue that since the benefit is not relevant to the actual effort decision, it must have been sufficiently large for her to take the credit. However, aggressive advertisement campaigns take advantage of the consumers who are near-sided or thoughtless in their dealings with credit contracts. When taking credit, these consumers lack an understanding of the relative merits of contracts available. Upon, receiving the "free t-shirt", they fail to consider the implications that the new credit has on future income. Often, once a consumer has become aware of her new credit liability, she may even increase effort above the efficient level in order to meet her debt obligation. On account of this effect, it is rational for the creditors to promote such contracts. A sufficient understanding of this problem requires more elaborate exploration of these effects. Some work carried out in this field, Bar-Gill (2004) uses a behavioral approach to explain several particular features of credit card contracts, claiming that benefit programs and high interest rates are used to take advantage of the consumers' chronic underestimation of future borrowings.

This glimpse into the approach offered by bounded rationality shows that it would be particularly rewarding to explore this approach further in a latter paper.

To sum up: Incorporating risk aversion into the original framework did not remove the ex-ante distortion created by the prospect of debt release. Yet, extending the framework it showed that the debtor is more willing to choose a higher effort level to avoid bankruptcy. The debtor most likely raises ex-ante precaution, even above the efficient level, if the credit contract leads to an increase in variance across income realizations. It is concluded, that maintaining ex-ante efficiency does not necessarily require one to give up the idea of debt release. The modifications exercised within the model did indicate that the debtor would raise ex-ante precautions for each case. The debtors incentives remained distorted under the Ch. 7 bankruptcy regulation. As found in Ch. 7, the debtor will be lax towards ex-ante effort when the expected discomfort is low.

5.7 Discussion

This section provides a critical assessment of the model's assumptions, interprets the results and points out possible extensions.

Occurrence of Distress

The circumstances of bankruptcy are modeled in a highly stylized way, with apparent simplifications. The debt payment is due at once and in full. The debtor's solvency rests entirely on a one-time realizations based upon a singular effort choice. As debt contracts are usually paid off gradually, distress is also an evolving process. Since the purpose of the analysis is not to provide a detailed investigation on how distress evolves, the present model provides an expedient approximation of the phenomenon. Individual histories leading to bankruptcy filing are diverse and complex. Therefore, the model confines itself to a mapping of the general effects.

The patterns of the bankruptcy regulation were shown to have a vital effect on the debtor's effort, which in turn, determines the default probability. Rather generous regulations may trigger negligent behavior. Moreover, it is observed that default usually occurs within the first two years of the contract[24] when the greater part of the debt obligation is still pending. This implies that either the debtor settles with debt payments and pays off the entire contract or she fails to accommodate with payments and default occurs at an early date. Hence, the model provides an adequate approximation, based on simplified assumptions.

Distress is more evolving than a sudden occurrence. Yet, once the debtor starts experiencing financial difficulty, she can seldom wrench herself out of that worsening situation by gambling for a large increase in income. She may restrict her consumption and increase her working efforts, but in general an individual consumer has little means augment income to that point. This differs from corporate bankruptcy, where a firm may tip venture back into a firm position by adopting some highly risky project.[25] Except for buying a lottery ticket, a consumer hardly faces equivalent possibilities. Still, a debtor may delay a bankruptcy filing or even culpably incur more

[24] see Schuldenkompass (2003)

[25] These projects usually promise a high return in case of success, yet rarely have a positive expected value. Hence, the risk is carried out manly on the expenses of the creditor. For an analysis see for example Stiglitz andWeiss (1981) and Bester and Hellwig (1989).

debt in the mean time.[26] This is often beneficial for the debtor, because her ability to pay is bounded, whereas the penalty does not rise with the amount defaulted upon. As a result, she may profit from increasing her expenditure before filing. Such end-game effects entail that credit is given to a consumer who did not genuinely afford it. A further exploration of this phenomenon would make an interesting extension. A study could be conducted on how a bankruptcy regulation channels such phenomena as consumption smoothing benefits, the shifting of assets and other forms of strategic behavior.

This analysis assumes a perfectly competitive credit market, which is taken for convenience. Even if creditors were able to charge an interest rate above the market rate it would not change the results of the analysis. The decision on taking the credit rested entirely upon the consumer's expected benefit, which is exogenous to the analysis. Extending the analysis to consider this decision would either lead to a consideration of boundedly rational debtors who overestimate the benefit of a credit; or it focuses fraudulent debtors who take credits they cannot afford. In both scenarios it may be explored whether the proposed regulation incentivises the debtor to take the proper decision, since she is the one who has the best knowledge about her expected future income.

Results

The ex-post analysis states that debt release is often inevitable, however, an immediate debt release - as possible under Ch. 7 - provides poor incentives from an ex-ante perspective. However, any kind of debt release is capable of distorting the debtor's choice ex-ante. Yet, it is shown that ex-ante distortions may occur even for unlimited liability (no debt release), particularly, if future income is sufficiently low. This is true generally for those consumers who expect to suffer little from the applicable regulations, that is that they expect little future wealth, or have little personal conviction towards default. However, such cases provoke doubt that giving the credit was a considerate decision in the first place. It may be concluded a moderate debt release regulation achieves a sufficient ex-ante threat that for most parameters while offering the defaulter ex-post a way out of debt. Moreover, when the analysis is extended to the broader consequences of

[26] This effect is known in the U.S. as consumption smoothing benefits. It was observed, for example, by Fisher and Filer (2002) that consumers tend to increase their consumption by 15% shortly before filing for bankruptcy.

bankruptcy, ex-ante distortions were mitigated. Also the consideration of risk aversion lessened ex-ante distortions. Yet, risk aversion can also produce the opposite effect. Consumers opt for credit that reduces variance in income even at a reduction to the net expected income. This is only possible when the bankruptcy regulation is sufficiently generous or the consumer expects to endure little punishment from the regulation. Yet, introducing the notion of bounded rationality suggested that the debtor's decision may be based on different considerations. When, for example, the benefit of the credit was consumed before the debtor starts working for payments, she is then mostly concerned about worsening her current situation. As a result, it may be said that ex-ante distortions are less severe than suspected.

Many scholars claim that bankruptcy regulation is particularly vulnerable to misuse by fraudulent debtors, suggesting that the regulation should distinguish between those and the unfortunate ones. In the paper, I refrained attempting to descry the debtor's motives, claiming that if the bankruptcy regulation offers little range for profiting, such distinctions are unnecessary. Hence, certain obstacles should be placed, before a debt release is to be granted. Two kind of obstacles are known in the various regulations. The first one aims at some kind of re-education of the debtor's attitude towards handling of credit and places certain non-monetary penalties on the debtor in order to teach her to not to default. As discussed, such regulations were shown to produce little additional return for the creditor while running the risk of distorting the debtor's economic incentives ex-post. Different types of debtors may face harsher distortions from this policy ex-ante. As, they may have a biased effect ex-ante as too much stigma deters 'honest' debtors from taking credit. It is found that the least distorting requirement is a fixed sum of money based on the debtor' capabilities (i.e. observe her participation constraint). This provides positive ex-ante effects, increasing the expected compensation of the creditor in case of default, while lowering the risk of default, by motivating the debtor to avoid default. Though distortions seem to persist, they were shown to be minimized to a reasonable parameter range under the proposed regulation.

Extensions

The analysis can be extended along several dimensions. As mentioned, the implications of the proposal may provide insight on the incentive to delay filing or to further explore the idea of bounded rationality. This model could be further applied to an entrepreneur's risk attitude shortly prior to bankruptcy. Again the provision of statistical data would strengthen the results, yet, as the analysis ranges across dissimilar jurisdictions such numbers would be of limited significance.

5.8 Results

This section sums up the results found in the ex-ante analysis.

(1) When the debtor is risk neutral any form of debt release causes ex-ante distortions. These distortions are higher when a lower penalty is imposed on the debtor in case of distress is. It was shown that of the four regulations considered, the proposal caused the least ex-ante distortions.
(2) Introducing possible extensions into the model gives biased results. The existence of a collateral does raise the debtor's ex-ante incentives, while the consideration of renegotiations may have biased effects as they ease the disutility experienced by the debtor.
(3) Changes in income expectations do not ease the problem of debt release for they change the reference point.
(4) Stigma has a twisted effect: Though it clearly aggravates the effects of an ex-post penalty, it may also deter honest individuals from taking credit at all.
(5) The introduction of risk-aversion did not improve results. Yet, some modifications, such as the bounded rationality, suggest that the debtor is more likely to raise precautions, even with the prospect of debt release. As a result, the prospect of debt release does not inevitably cause ex-ante distortions.

Chapter 6

Ex-Ante vs. Ex-Post Efficiency

This section places the results of the formal analysis into a broader context. Here, the analysis of both the ex-ante and ex-post chapters are infused to further theory on consumer bankruptcy regulation. Based on this understanding of consumer bankruptcy regulation a new regulation is proposed. This proposal provides an alternative second-best solution which best minimizes the distortions in the present set-up.

Consumer credit enables an individual to smooth consumption over time, thereby, shifting it to the most rewarding period. Yet, when income realizations turn out to be low, the consumer experiences difficulty in meeting her credit obligation. This raises the necessity of a regulated debt release, as the absence of such causes a welfare loss since the consumer may be deterred from further economic activity. Using a hidden action model, I analyzed the prominent features of bankruptcy regulations, and pointed out prevailing inefficiencies. Based on these findings, I propose a regulation which - within the assumptions of the model - outperforms all existing regulations. This provides a guideline to be used for setting a particular amount of repayment as the prerequisite for debt release. This amount is set in proportion to the debtor's abilities, as -due to distress- her capacity is bounded.

A perfect bankruptcy regime would not alter the debtor's working incentive post filing. Likewise, her ex-ante choices should not should be affected by the existence of a credit contract, or more perceives by the prospect of debt release, since credit taken for consumer goods does not change income expectations. The ex-post analysis of chapter 4, identified various inefficiencies that impair the incentives of the debtor, once she has filed for bankruptcy.

The accomplishment of the existing rules has been poor. Under **Ch. 7**, the assets are taken and the remaining penalty is zero- the creditor will not receive the amount owed unless it was equal to the value of seized assets. In the German regulation (pre 99'), the debtor will also not re-pay for she is completely overwhelmed. Ex-post disincentives were also found in the current German regulation (post 99'), the debtor has no incentive to work hard to repay debts when she does not receive any kick-back for doing so. A reformed regulation was proposed, which strives to solve these inefficiencies . The debtor's choices were shown to be guided by two conditions, her willingness to participate and the incentives to exert herself. A fixed sum, based on the debtor's ability, was shown to improve upon both conditions, by leaving the debtor as the residual claimant. The magnitude of this amount should either be set equal to the outstanding debt itself or to sum, P^{max}, which is derived from the participation constraint. This P^{max} reduces the debtor to her reservation utility.

Later in chapter 4, the inter-temporal component was added to the analysis. Consideration is given to the variance in income realizations may be accounted for if the debtor makes her choices sequentially. What is found is that because income realizations vary, the debtor's participation constraint may cease to hold at later dates, resulting in the debtor's abstention. This consideration calls for an adjustment of the maximum amount, granting some surplus to the debtor. Hence, to derive a general rule that sets optimal incentives for most parameters, it is sensible to array P^{max} to the debtor's expected income for a certain number of years, e.g. six as the German regulation suggests, $P = 6y_{th}$. Depending on the variance of income realization the actual duration of the period of payment may vary between three and ten years. The variance depends mostly on the debtor's latitude to influence income realizations and partly on exogenous circumstances. Still, it is sensible to have a hardship discharge or some regulation on the maximum length of the period of good conduct, as it balances undue pressure upon the incentive compatibility of the regulation. Adding risk-aversion into the analysis (section 4.3.2) did not significantly alter the results.

The relative merits of three additional proposals were considered (4.4.1-4.4.3). These three proposals comprise the inclusion of a variable period of good conduct, partial garnishment, and a period of supervision. Following, a case was made as to why the proposal made for this paper is superior to each of the three regulations.

Testing the proposed rule for ex-ante incentive effects, namely on the debtor's incentive to avoid distress, it transpires that any kind of debt release will incentivize the debtor to lower ex-ante precaution. Yet, the proposed regulation is shown to cause the least distortions of all considered regulations, even compared to unlimited liability rule. Since the proposed regulation overcomes the ex-post welfare loss created by limited liability, the creditor can always expect some compensation. Hence, the proposed regulation achieves ex-post efficiency while at the same time minimizing ex-ante distortions. Several extensions such as the existence of a collateral and a change in income expectations did not alleviate the observed distortion. Social stigma turned out to have a biased effect. The introduction of classic risk aversion did not absolve the identified trade off. Yet, a broadened setup suggested that a debtor increases her precaution when taking credit. In particular, when the credit's benefit is short lived, she may end up working harder, since she is left with the costs. This shifts her income realizations to a lower region, which increases the marginal benefits of her effort. Similar results were obtained when introducing the notion of bounded rationality. Here, the consumer discarded all components common to the offered prospects. The debtor has distinct risk attitudes for losses and gains under bounded rationality , being more sensitive to loss than a gain of equal magnitude. Applying this theory, resulted in only marginal distortions.

These considerations suggest that the persistent trade-off between ex-ante and ex-post efficiency, namely that any kind of debt release causes ex-ante distortions, is less imminent than prior results suggest. The debtor is likely to take sufficient precaution against distress even when she expects some debt release. To put it in a nutshell: When the regulation causes sufficient inconvenience, the debtor will be sufficiently cautious. Equally, mitigations are better achieved, when the creditor's expected compensation is higher. Yet, from an ex-post perspective a regulated debt release is inevitable, as otherwise the debtor's incentives could be gravely distorted. The proposal offers a sophisticated debt release regulation that provides an adequately balances efficiency requirements at both dates.

Chapter 7
Conclusion

During the last decade, several European countries identified the need for consumer debt release regulation, and amended their bankruptcy codes accordingly, allowing consumers and other non-business entities to petition for debt discharge. The devices, which qualify the consumer for a debt discharge can be grouped into three categories: seizure of current assets, garnishment of future income and other non-monetary penalties. The paper explicitly integrates the ex-post limits of liability into the analysis of credit contracts. The analysis has shown that debt release is an inevitable property of a bankruptcy regime ex-post. However, this necessity is likely to create distortions in the debtor's ex-ante choice. Recognizing such impeding distortions, many bankruptcy codes pose several obstacles in the debtor's way to debt release. One possibility is non-monetary penalties, which can be found, for example, in the British regulation or in many other common wealth countries.

The simple multiple period model used in this paper was capable of an analysis of bankruptcy regulations from various jurisdictions the ex-ante and ex-post incentive structure of four exemplary bankruptcy regulations was analyzed.

Though an unlimited liability regime is usually thought to provide optimal ex-ante incentives, it shows that such a regime may seriously distort the debtor's economic incentives ex-post. Debt release seems to be a desirable and inevitable tool for a bankruptcy code.

Many of the existing regulations were shown to distort the individual debtor's effort choice ex-post, as these pay little attention to the debtor's incentives during the period of good conduct and her financial capabilities.

Existing regulations does not pay insufficient attention to these matters. A rule was developed, which implements the optimal effort and also increases the collection rate of the creditors. The results are shown to be stable to the introduction of risk aversion.

The effects of the regulations on consumer decisions prior to distress are considered in the ex-ante analysis. It is shown that the harder the regulation, the better the ex-ante incentives are. Generally any kind of debt discharge has negative effects on the debtor's performance, but the debtor's choices may be distorted even in the absence of a debt release. This effect is likely to result in credit rationing and an increase in the interest rate. Distortions were mitigated when accounting for risk aversion and almost vanish when applying bounded rationality. To conclude, a sophisticated debt discharge regulation for consumers is a desirable feature of a bankruptcy code.

Bibliography

Ackerlof, George, The Market for Lemons: Quality Uncertainty and the Market Mechansim (1970) Quaterly Journal of Economics Vol. 89, pp. 488-500.

Adler, Barry, Ben Polak and Alan Schwartz, Regulating Consumer Bankruptcy: A Theoretical Inquiry (2000) Journal of Legal Studies Vol. 29, pp. 585-613.

Aghion, Philippe, Bankruptcy and its Reforms (1998) in: P. Newman (ed.): The New Palgrave Dictionary of Economics and the Law, Vol. 3, pp. 405-410.

Alexopoulos, Michelle and Ian Domowitz, Personal Liabilities and Bankruptcy Reform: An International Perspective (1998) International Finance Vol. 1 No. 1, pp 127-139.

Athreya, Kartik, Welfare Implications of the Bankruptcy Reform Act of 1999 (2002) Journal of Monetary Economics Vol. 49, pp. 1567-1595.

Bar-Gill, Oren, Seduction by Plastic (2004) Paper presented at the Annual Meeting of the American Law & Economics Association 2004, No. 12, pp. 1-66.

Berkowitz, Jeremy and Richard Hynes, Bankruptcy Exemption and the Market for Mortgage Loans (1999) Journal of Law and Economics Vol. 42, pp. 809-829.

Berkowitz, Jeremy and Michelle J. White, Bankruptcy and Small Firms' Access to Credit (2002) NBER working paper, pp. 1-26.

Bhandari, Jagdeep S. and Lawrence A. Weiss, Corporate Bankruptcy (1996), Cambridge University Press, London.

Berliner Senatsverwaltung für Arbeit Soziales und Frauen, Entwicklung der Schuldner- und Insolvenzberatung im Land Berlin nach Inkrafttreten der Verbraucherinsolvenz (2000) Berlin, p. 7.

Bester, Helmut and Martin Hellwig, Moral Hazard and Equilibrium Credit Rationing, (1989) in: Bamberg/Spremann (eds.): Agency Theory, Information, and Incentives, Berlin, Heidelberg 1989, pp. 135-166.

Bigus, Jochen and Eva-Maria Steiger, When it Pays to be Honest: How a Variable Period of Good Conduct can Improve Incentives in Personal Bankruptcy Proceedings (2002), paper presented at the Annual Meeting of the American

Law and Economics Association 2002.

Bigus, Jochen and Eva-Maria Steiger, Variable Wohlverhaltensperiode als anreizkompatibles Instrument des Verbraucherinsolvenzverfahrens (2003), Zeitschrift für Betriebswirtsschaft Vol. 73, pp. 1197-1219.

Bolton, Patrick and David Scharfstein, A Theory of Predation Based on Agency Problems in Financial Contracting (1990) American Economic Review Vol. 80, pp. 93-106.

Brockman, Chris, Bankruptcy - a fresh start? (2004) New Law Journal, pp. 488-89.

Bund - Länder - Arbeitsgruppe Inslovenzrecht, Probleme bei der praktischen Anwendung und Schwachstellen des Verbraucherinsolvenzverfahrens, Analyse und Änderungsvorschläfe (2000) Bericht zur 71. Konferenz der Justizministerinnen und Justizminister am 24. und 25. Mai 2000 in Potsdam.

Culhane, Marianne B. and Michaela M. White, Debt after Discharge: an Empirical Study of Reaffirmation (1999) American Bankruptcy Law Journal Vol. 73, pp. 709-774.

Czarnetzky, John M., The Individual and Failure: a Theory of the Bankruptcy Discharge (2000) Arizona State Law Journal Vol. 32, pp. 393-464.

Draper, Hal, The Complete Poems of Heinrich Heine: A Modern English Version (1982) Suhrkamp/Insel, Publisher Boston, Inc., p. 79.

Efrat, Rafael, The Moral Appeal of Persoanl Bankruptcy (1998) Whittier Law Review Vol 20, pp. 141-67.

Efrat, Rafael, Global Trends in Personal Bankruptcy (2001) Working paper presented at Winter Leadership Conference, Carlsbad CA http://www.abiworld.org/abidata/online/conference/01wlc/Efrat.html.

Fay, Scott, Erik Hurst and Michelle J. White, The household Bankruptcy Decision (2002) American Economic Review Vol. 92 No. 3, pp.706-718.

Filer, Larry and Jonathan Fisher, The Consumption Effects Associated with Filing for Personal Bankruptcy (2002) Paper presented at the Anual Meeting of the American Law and Economics Association, pp. 1-36.

Fishburn, P.C., Mean-Risk Analysis with Risk Associatied with Below-Target Returns (1977), American Economic Review Vol. 67, pp. 116-126.

Fisher, Jonathan, Larry Filer ad Angela Lyons, Is the Bankruptcy Flag Binding? Access to Credit Markets for Post-Banrkuptcy Households (2004) American Law & Economics Associaiton Annual Meetings Paper 28, pp.1-19.

Forsblad, Kirsten, Restschuldbefreiung und Verbraucherinsolvenz im künftigen deutschen Insolvenzrecht (1997) Berlin et al. 1997, Diss, Göttingen 1997.

Fruhner, F-M, Die Novelle zum Verbraucherinsolvenzverfahren (2002) NJ, pp 11-14.

Gale, Douglas and Martin Hellwig, Incentive-Compatible Contracts: The One-Period Problem (1985) Review of Economic Studies Vol. 52, pp. 647-63.

Graver, Hans Peter, Consumer Bankruptcy: A Right or a Privilege? The Role of the Courts in Establishing Moral Standards of Economic Conduct (1997) Journal of Consumer Policy Vol. 20, pp. 161-177.

Gropp, Reint, John Karl Scholz and Michelle J. White, Personal Bankruptcy and Credit Supply and Demand (1997) 112 Quarterly Journal of Economics 217.

Han, Song and Wenli Li, Fresh Start or Head Start? The Effect of Filing for Bankruptcy on the Labor Supply (2004) FRB of Philadelphia Working Paper No. 04-5.

Hess, Harald, Rüdiger Wienberg and Patricia Titze-Fischer, Zur Notwendigkeit einer Reform des Verbraucherinsolvenzverfahrens (2000) NZI Neue Zeitschrift für das Recht der Insolvenz und Sanierung Vol. 3/2000, pp. 97-102.

Holzhammer, Richard, Österreichisches Insolvenzrecht, Konkurs und Ausgleich (1996), Springer Verlag

Huls, Nick, Overindebtedness and Overlegalization: Consumer Bankruptcy as a Field for Alternative Dispute Resolution (1997) Journal of Consumer Policy Vol. 20, pp. 143-159.

Hynes, Richard and Eric A. Posner, The Law and Economics of Consumer Finance (2002) American Law and Economics Review Vol. 4 No. 1, pp.168-207.

Innes, Robert D., Limited Liabitlity and Incentive Contracting with Ex-ante Action Choices (1990) Journal of Economic Theory Vol. 52, pp. 45-67.

Iversen, Bent, Jorgen Norgaard, Lars Lindencrone Petersen and Morten Wegener, Danish Business Law (2000) , pp. 439-441.

Jackson, T., The Logic and Limits of Bankruptcy Law (1986) Cambridge MA: Harvard University Press.

Jacoby, Melissa, Collecting Debts from the ill and injured: the Rhetorical Significance, but Practical Irrelevance, of Culpability and Ability to Pay (2002) American University Law Review Vol. 51, pp. 229-271.

Jeweler, Robin, The "Bankruptcy Abuse Prevention and Consumer Protection Act of 2005," S. 256, in the 109th Congress (2005) CRS Report for the Congress, RL 32765.

Kahneman, Daniel and Amos Tversky, Prospect Theory: An Analysis of Decision under Risk (1979) Economiertica Vol 47 No. 2, pp. 263-291.

Krüger, Ulrich, Alternative Konfliktregelung un d Verbraucherinsolvenzverfahren (2000) NZI Neue Zeitschrift für das Recht der Insolvenz und Sanierung Vol. 4/2000, pp. 151-160.

Kübler, Bruno M. and Hanns Prütting, Das neue Insolvenzrecht: 2 Bände: - InsO/EGInsO (Band 1) (1994) , pp. 227-242, 529-542

Mas-Colell, Andreu, Michael D. Whinston and Jerry R. Green, Microeconomic Theory (1995) Oxford University Press, New York.

McGregor, Brigitta Kilingander and Jean Lown, Comparative Analysis of Canadian, American and Swedish Bankruptcy Policy: Why do Goverments legislate consumer debt? (2001) International Journal of Consumer Studies, Vol. 25, No. 3, pp. 208-227.

Musto, David, The Reaquistion of Credit following Chapter 7 Personal Bankruptcy (1999) Working Paper 99-22,

http://knowledge.wharton.upenn.edu/PDFs/890.pdf, pp. 1-35.
National Bankruptcy Review Comission, Report (1997) http://govinfo.library.unt.edu/nbrc/reporttitlepg.html.
Niemi-Kiesiläinen, Johanna, Changing Directions in Consumer Bankruptcy Law and Practice in Europe and U.S.A. (1997) Journal of Consumer Policy Vol. 20, pp. 133-142.
Posner, Eric A., Should Debtors be Forced into Chapter 13?, (1999), Loyola of Los Angeles Law Review, Vol. 32, pp. 965-976.
Price, Zachary, The Bankruptcy Abuse Prevention and Consumer Protection Act (2002) Harvard Journal on Legislation Vol 39, pp. 237-254.
Ramsay, Ian, Models of Consumer Bankruptcy: Implications for Research and Policy (1997) Journal of Consumer Policy Vol. 20, pp. 269-287.
Robe, Michel A., Optimal vs. Traditional Securities under Moral Hazard (1999) Journal of Financial and Quantitative Analysis Vol. 34, No. 2, pp. 161-189.
Robe, Michel A., Pierre-Armand Michel, Penalties and Optimality in Financial Contracts Taking Stock (2002) Working Paper, pp. 1-25.
Rubinstein, Ariel, Modeling Bounded Rationality (1998), MIT Press Cambridge, Massachusetts.
SCHUFA Holding AG (Hrsg.), Schulden-Kompass 2003: Empirische Indikatoren der privaten Ver- und Überschuldung in Deutschland (2003), Schufa Wiesbaden.
Selten, Reinhard, What is Bounded Rationality? (2001) in Gegerrenze and Selten (eds.) Bounded Rationality: The Adaptive Tool Box, Cambridge and London MIT Press, pp. 13-36.
Sullivan, T.A., E. Warren and J.L. Westerbrook, Consumer bankruptcy in the United States: A study of alleged abuse and of local legal culture (1997) Journal of Consumer Policy Vol. 20, pp. 223-268.
Stiglitz, Joseph E. and Andrew Weiss, Credit Rationing in Markets with Imperfect Information (1981) American Economic Review Vol. 71, No.3, pp. 393-410.
Trendelenburg, Hortense, Restschuldbefreiung (2000) Baden-Baden 2000, Diss. Uni Leipzig 1999.
Wang, Hung-Jen, Michelle J. White, An Optimal Personal Bankruptcy Procedure and Proposed Reforms (2000) Journal of Legal Studies Vol. 29, pp. 255-286.
Weiss, Lawrence A., Jagdeep S. Bhandari, Russell Robins, An Analysis of State-Wide Variation in Bankruptcy Rates in the United States (2001) Bankruptcy Developments Journal Vol. 17, pp. 407-424.
White, Michelle J., Why it Pays to File for Bankruptcy: A critical Look at the Incentives under U.S. Personal Bankruptcy Law and a Proposal for Change (1998) University of Chicago Law Review Vol. 65, pp. 685-732.
White, Michelle J., Why Don't More Households File for Bankruptcy? (1998a) Journal of Law Economics and Organization Vol. 14 No. 2, pp. 205-231.
Whitford, William C., Changing Definitions of Fresh Start in U.S. Bankruptcy Law (1997) Journal of Consumer Policy Vol. 20, pp. 179-198.

Zaborowski, Christoph, Peter Zweifel, Getting out of Debt: Garnishment of Wage in Whose Interest? (1999) European Journal of Law and Economics Vol. 8, pp. 207-230.

GPSR Compliance

The European Union's (EU) General Product Safety Regulation (GPSR) is a set of rules that requires consumer products to be safe and our obligations to ensure this.

If you have any concerns about our products, you can contact us on ProductSafety@springernature.com

In case Publisher is established outside the EU, the EU authorized representative is:

Springer Nature Customer Service Center GmbH
Europaplatz 3
69115 Heidelberg, Germany

Batch number: 10725993

Printed by Printforce, the Netherlands